The Sky's the Limit – Access your online resources

The Sky's the Limit is accompanied by a number of printable online materials, designed to ensure this resource best supports your professional needs.

Activate your resources in three simple steps:

- Go to www.speechmark.net then create account / login

- Once registered, go to My Resources, where you'll be asked to enter the below activation code

- Once activated, all online resources that accompany The Sky's the Limit will appear in the My Resources section of your account – every time you log in

ACTIVATION CODE* –

rbsjikekhg

id:165

*Note, activation codes may be used on a one time only basis

A number of new Speechmark titles are accompanied by supporting materials, accessible online. Each time you purchase one, enter your unique activation code (typically found on the inside front cover of the resource) and enjoy access to My Resources – your very own online library of printable, practical resources that may be accessed again and again.

The Sky's the Limit

A Workbook for Teaching Mental Wellbeing to Young People with SEN

Victoria Honeybourne

Speechmark

To Marilyn, for showing me what's possible.

First published in 2016 by
Speechmark Publishing Ltd, 2nd Floor,
5 Thomas More Square, London E1W 1YW, UK
Tel: +44 (0)845 034 4610 Fax: +44 (0)845 034 4649
www.speechmark.net

Designed and typeset by Moo Creative (Luton)

002-6018/Printed in the United Kingdom by CMP (uk) Ltd

British Library Cataloguing in Publication Data
A catalogue record for this book is available from the British Library

ISBN 978 190930 170 2

Contents

Acknowledgements

Big thanks to Neil Vanes for his illustrations and to Clare Baldrey and Rachel Makey for their feedback during the writing process. Also, this resource would not have been created without a fantastic group of students who questioned, challenged and helped to refine the activities: Ben, Cam, Joe, Laura, Liam, Ryan, Shaun and Steffan.

Note from the author

I finished primary school, aged eleven, with a glowing report card: 'For Victoria, the sky's the limit!' the Head Teacher had concluded in her comments. For a good time after this, I believed that Head Teacher must have got it wrong. The sky certainly didn't seem to be the limit. As I became a teenager and young adult, I felt limited by so many things, especially my low self-esteem, lack of self-awareness and limited emotional intelligence.

It was only 20 years later, after receiving some excellent support to work on my self-esteem and self-awareness, that I began to believe that the Head Teacher may have got it right after all.

As a teacher of SEN, I have seen many young people with learning or communication difficulties struggle to understand the abstract concept of mental wellbeing and experiencing low self-esteem, depression, isolation and other problems which can continue to exist into adulthood.

This resource developed from successful teaching sessions I have led with young people with a range of needs. I hope that publishing this will enable many other young people to understand how they can improve their mental wellbeing and to realise that for them, too, the sky really is the limit.

Victoria Honeybourne
(June 2015)

Introduction for adults

Overview

This book originally developed out of resources and activities used when I was working in the classroom with young people who had a range of special educational needs (SEN). As a teacher, I was seeking a method of transforming the rather abstract concept of mental wellbeing to something more concrete and visual. Many students felt sad or worried, could not identify why and could not imagine what they could do to help themselves feel better. Other students were asking difficult questions, such as 'Why are some people happy all of the time but I'm not?' or 'If my parents are depressed, does that mean I will be too when I grow up?'

Over time I, along with my group of students, developed a visual analogy along with a child-friendly narrative. In this visual, various flying objects explained why they could fly easily on some days but felt stuck on the ground at other times. This analogy enabled students to 'see' what was meant by mental wellbeing and created an accessible way of expressing and discussing feelings for students with communication difficulties.

This book is divided into two parts: the first is a short 'story' in the form of cartoons, using the sky as a setting and flying objects as characters; the second contains corresponding activities and worksheets for adults to use with young people to enable them to develop further their understanding and self-awareness.

Aims of this book

In today's fast-paced society and times of economic uncertainty, mental wellbeing has never been more important. Children who are mentally healthy are able to develop psychologically, emotionally and intellectually, which is essential for both academic and personal success. 'Mental wellbeing' includes having a sense of personal identity, the ability to get on with other people and the ability to cope with everyday problems.

The aims of this resource are:

- To provide a visual analogy which enables children and young people with special educational needs to express and discuss their mental wellbeing through
    o establishing a personal identity
    o increasing self-esteem
    o identifying, labelling and learning to self-regulate emotions
    o developing increased resilience and the confidence to approach challenges and new experiences.

- To provide information and activities for teachers and other adults to enable them to feel increasingly confident in exploring concepts of mental wellbeing with young people.

- To use methods and techniques from the field of positive psychology to create a solution-focused approach.

Who this book is for

This resource has been designed to be easily used by anyone working with children or young people in a range of settings: teachers, teaching assistants, support workers, professionals from various fields, or parents and carers. There is currently a scarcity of psychologists and accredited therapists to work with young people (Greig & Mackay, 2013) and this resource is intended to be used as an early intervention or preventive strategy in schools or other settings. It is also intended as an empowering tool which enables young people to express their feelings and learn about themselves, rather than a tool which intends to 'solve' or 'fix' mental health difficulties.

These materials are designed to be accessible to people without any specific training. The most important things for adults to bring to the sessions are a non-judgemental attitude and a willingness to allow the young people in question to take ownership and develop their own solutions.

The activities were originally developed with young people with communication difficulties and special educational needs at Key Stages 3 and 4 (11–16 years).The students involved had a range of identified needs, including speech and language difficulties, autism spectrum conditions, ADHD and social and emotional difficulties. However, the resource is designed to be flexible enough to work with a wide range of young people from Key Stage 1 (5–7 years) onwards.

The particular groups of students who may benefit are:

- those with identified communication difficulties or special educational needs (eg receptive or expressive language difficulties; speech, language and communication needs; specific language impairment; autism spectrum conditions; moderate learning difficulties; ADHD)

- students with low self-esteem

- vulnerable or anxious students who may be at risk of becoming isolated, marginalised or bullied

- students who are anxious about the transition from primary to secondary school

- students at risk of developing mental health difficulties.

Inevitably, there will be young people who require a higher level of support from mental health professionals. However, this resource can help to complement that work by supporting students to gain some of the communication skills which will enable them to interact more confidently with other professionals.

It is not uncommon for children and young people to experience mental health difficulties. Only a minority will go on to experience severe, long-lasting or multiple difficulties. These can have a huge impact on the individuals, their families and their education. If you are concerned about a young person's mental health, seek support as soon as possible. The services available will differ from area to area. Your school's special educational needs co-ordinator (SENCo), nurse, counsellor or pastoral leader can often direct or refer you to the most suitable service, from the statutory, voluntary or school-based sector, as can the child's doctor. Parents and carers may also need support to help them cope with a young person's mental health needs – many organisations can offer this support too.

In the UK, specialist CAMHS (child and adolescent mental health services) are NHS (National Health Service) mental health services that meet the needs of children and young people. They are multidisciplinary teams consisting of psychiatrists, psychologists, social workers, therapists, support workers and specialist workers. Referral procedures differ from area to area and most local CAMHS have their own website. There is a list of further resources at the end of this Introduction.

How to use this book

This resource is designed to be used with either individuals or small groups of a maximum of six students. Several activities can also be adapted for whole-class use and these are identified in the text where appropriate.

Part 1 is a visual short story. Although some students may wish and be able to read this independently, it is envisaged that most students will work through the story with an adult, using the narrative as a vehicle to prompt further discussion. Some students with learning difficulties will benefit from frequent repetition of the story.

Part 2 contains the corresponding activities to develop students' understanding of the issues covered in Part 1. Each activity begins with notes for the teacher or adult, explaining what the activity intends to do, how the activity can be adapted to extend or support different students, and suggesting variations on how to deliver the activity. Adults can choose the most suitable method for their group of students. Some students may prefer to complete the activities using a computer and should be encouraged to choose the form of communication they are most comfortable with.

This resource is not prescriptive: how much is covered in each session depends very much on the size of the group, the ability and concentration of the students, and the length of each session. Some activities are designed to be completed in one session while others require reflection in other situations between sessions. The amount of time to spend on each activity is not specified because children and young people, especially those with special educational needs, are likely to learn in individual ways and some will need to spend more time on certain topics than others.

It is important to remember that this resource will have the greatest impact if frequent links are made to everyday situations and if it is made explicit to students how they can apply the skills they are learning to situations in the mainstream classroom or at home. Involving all of the staff who work with the children and young people, as well as parents or carers, can have the greatest impact, as effective strategies can be reinforced. Most of the activities are not intended to be stand-alone, one-off activities; they introduce strategies and ideas which students can use on an ongoing basis.

Why this book is needed

❝ *We all play a part in helping children and young people grow up. Mental health and psychological well-being are not the preserve of one profession or another, or of one government department or another. ...*

***Anyone in contact with a child has an impact on that child's mental health and psychological well-being. The challenge for all of us is to remember that and to be able to respond if things start to go wrong.* ❞**

(Jo Davidson, Chair National CAMHS Review, 2008, p6)

Mental wellbeing

Mental wellbeing is a current government, health, social and educational priority and the paucity of readily available support and resources is well documented. As the statistics that follow show, mental health difficulties are an issue for a growing number of young people and early intervention is essential.

1 in 10 children and young people aged 5 – 16 suffer from a diagnosable mental health disorder – that is around three children in every class.

More than half of all adults with mental health problems were diagnosed in childhood. Less than half were treated appropriately at the time.

Nearly 80,000 children and young people suffer from severe depression.

72% of children in care have behavioural or emotional problems – these are some of the most vulnerable people in our society.

Between 1 in every 12 and 1 in 15 children and young people deliberately self-harm.

95% of imprisoned young offenders have a mental health disorder. Many of them are struggling with more than one disorder.

The number of young people aged 15–16 with depression nearly doubled between the 1980s and the 2000s.

There has been a high 68% increase in the number of young people being admitted to hospital because of self-harm over the past ten years.

(*Source*: YoungMinds, 2015)

There is no single cause of mental health difficulties and many genetic, socio-economic, environmental and psychological factors can be involved. School-related problems are also frequently cited by children and young people as contributing to mental health difficulties: bullying, learning difficulties, peer relationships and school-related anxieties. The impact of these concerns can vary from mild to acute, depending on the individual.

Mental health difficulties can often be linked with educational failure, family disruption, disability, offending and anti-social behaviour. If these difficulties are not supported in childhood and adolescence, they can continue into adulthood (McGirl, 2009).

Risk factors

Some individuals or groups can be more vulnerable to mental health difficulties than others. Some examples of the risk factors are listed opposite.

Risk factors in the child or young person	Risk factors in the family	Risk factors in the community
Specific learning difficulties	Parental conflict	Socio-economic disadvantage
Communication difficulties	Family breakdown	Homelessness
Specific developmental delay	Inconsistent, unclear discipline	Disaster
Genetic influence	Hostile rejecting relationships	Discrimination
Difficult temperament	Physical illness, especially chronic or neurological	Other significant events
Academic failure	Failure to adapt to child's changing needs	
Low self-esteem	Physical, sexual or emotional abuse	
	Parental psychiatric illness	
	Parental criminality, alcoholism or personality disorder	
	Death and loss – including friendship	

(Source: adapted from DfEE, 2001)

Some evidence suggests that children and young people with special educational needs can be up to six times more likely to experience mental health difficulties than their peers (NASS, 2015). In addition to experiencing low self-esteem, feeling vulnerable, left out, 'different' or isolated, children and young people with SEN can also find it more difficult than their peers to make and maintain social relationships, build friendships and participate in the community. All of these factors have been shown to be important in maintaining mental health.

Difficulties for children and young people with SEN in achieving mental wellbeing

Mental health difficulties can affect anyone and individuals often use a combination of methods to overcome these difficulties, depending on the nature and severity of the problem. These methods include:

- talking therapies

- chatting about problems with family or friends

- self-help books

- support groups, either in person or online

- mentoring or coaching

- medication

- making lifestyle changes.

Many people build up a 'bank' of self-help strategies (often without even realising) which help them to cope in difficult situations and maintain a sense of mental wellbeing. Such strategies can include:

- talking to supportive friends and family

- recording their thoughts and feelings, or keeping a journal

- looking for appropriate advice online or in books

- engaging in hobbies and interests they enjoy

- making necessary lifestyle changes

- identifying problems and working to solve these

- setting goals and identifying how to work towards them

- taking part in relaxation activities or meditation

- focusing on positives

- making a conscious effort to recognise negative thought cycles

- keeping healthy and rested.

However, for children and young people with special educational needs, using these types of strategy is sometimes not so easy. This section looks at some specific needs and the barriers these can create when establishing a sense of mental wellbeing.

Dyslexia-type difficulties or low literacy levels

Children with a low reading age may find it difficult to access written information (books, leaflets, posters, websites and emails). They may miss out on information given to other students, be unaware of the support available, and be unable to research independently. As well as missing useful information, this can also lead to feelings of frustration or even anger, as students may feel left behind or be unable to solve problems quickly.

> *Jamie is dyslexic and can't read an email her science teacher has sent to the class. She doesn't read the part about which topic next week's test is on, so she panics and tries to revise everything. She becomes worried about the test and even more frustrated when she realises that she has spent so much time revising topics which are not on the test.*

Top tips

- Ensure that all information, especially that regarding wellbeing and support, is given orally (eg in assemblies and in class) as well as in written form (because some students may not understand and remember information given orally)

- When giving out leaflets or letters containing useful information, read the text aloud to the students first. This will ensure that they know what information they have been given, rather than disregarding the paper immediately as meaningless. Ensure that students highlight key information so that they can find it easily (eg times of exams, useful websites).

- Teach students how to use text-voice software and screen readers. These are now available free of charge on most computers, tablets and smartphones. Students can then listen to information on websites instead of having to read it, thereby increasing their independence.

> *Taylor is becoming very upset about problems at home. She would like to speak to somebody but does not know who she can talk to. There are posters up in every classroom about where to find the school counsellor, but she can't read them.*

Receptive language difficulties

Children and young people with receptive language difficulties struggle to understand what is being said to them. They may have difficulty not only with items of vocabulary but also with understanding sentence construction (eg tenses, conjunctions) and with following a longer narrative. This can lead to difficulties such as: appearing not to follow instructions, so getting into trouble or doing the wrong thing; missing key information; feeling confused as they often 'get the wrong end of the stick' or don't understand what is going on. Many students with receptive language difficulties can go unnoticed and develop effective strategies to hide their difficulties. They may look like they are listening attentively, follow what other students are doing, avoid answering questions, or try to steer the conversation back to topics they are sure of. Receptive language difficulties can mean that students may not understand what people are saying to them or what they are being told about wellbeing.

> *Mr Marsh tells the class: 'You can go out to play if you have finished ten sums'. Joe runs outside immediately and doesn't understand why he is in trouble. Joe gets frustrated and angry as he didn't think he was doing anything wrong. This always seems to happen! He doesn't understand the meaning of conjunctions such as 'if'.*

Top tips

- Keep your language clear and simple. Don't avoid using longer vocabulary, but explain what new words mean.

- Keep sentences short and leave plenty of processing time for students to understand and make sense of what has been said.

- Check understanding regularly by asking students to explain what they have understood in their own words. Look out for students who repeat your words verbatim – they may not actually understand what they are saying.

- Provide visual support wherever possible. This ensures that students have something to 'hang' the language on and are on the right track. You could use concrete objects, photographs, pictures, videos, diagrams, gesture and role play to back up your message.

- Students with receptive language difficulties will also have the same difficulties understanding written information. Ensure that written materials provided are at a suitable level for the child to understand.

Expressive language difficulties

Children and young people with expressive language difficulties struggle to express themselves and to say what they mean. This can include difficulties with word finding, sentence construction or creating longer, coherent narratives. They can find it difficult to express how they feel or what has happened to them. It can be difficult

Speechmark ⑤

for them to explain exactly what the problem is and they may even appear to be telling lies or making things up. In lessons students may work hard but be unable to show what they know. This can damage self-esteem and may cause students to feel disheartened and to disengage.

Top tips

- Allow students to express themselves through different means (eg drawing, painting, modelling, making animations, making videos, taking photographs, using drama, using building bricks).

- Students may be able to express themselves better if they have small drawings or a cartoon strip to refer to. This can help them to put things in the right order and ensure they do not leave anything out.

- If a pupil is telling you a long, rambling story which doesn't make sense, you could try drawing it out with stick figures and speech bubbles as they are talking. Check with the pupil that you are drawing what happened accurately. It may then be easier to identify exactly what happened and who said what.

- Tell a pupil which parts you have understood and which parts you would like them to explain again.

- Some students will benefit from being taught the parts of speech (eg nouns, verbs) and how sentences are constructed.

Difficulties with time sequencing and concepts

Many children and young people with dyslexia or speech and language difficulties have associated difficulties with sequencing and time concepts. This can include:

- telling the time

- putting days, months and seasons in order

- understanding how long has passed ('I'll be back in 20 minutes' – what does 20 minutes feel like?)

- understanding concepts such as before and after

- understanding the sequence of the school day

- learning everyday sequences and patterns

- organising their work.

Being 'lost in time' can create a sense of confusion and unpredictability. In addition, it can make it much more difficult to plan effectively, set goals, solve problems and plan for the future.

> Samira is getting extremely anxious about her upcoming exams, which she says are 'in just a couple of weeks'. It is December and her exams are in June; however, she is not yet able to understand the sequence of months and times of year.
>
> A 12-year-old student is becoming extremely agitated at his teacher who has not yet phoned his mother about a change to the pick-up arrangements that afternoon. It is only 9 a.m. 'But my mum will be leaving the house soon to come and collect me and I'm meant to be going to football. It will be too late, she'll already be on her way. You need to phone her now!'
>
> A group of students were told to 'come back in twenty minutes' at lunchtime to pay in their school trip money. They didn't know if this would give them enough time to buy their lunch, so they waited instead and, by the time they had paid in their money, the canteen was closing.

Top tips

- Use visual timetables in school to support students in understanding the sequence of the school day. This can also be a chance to reduce anxiety about upcoming events.

- Use task boards to show the order of steps within a larger task.

- Teach students how to use their school planners, diaries and timetables most effectively.

- Sand-timers can be a useful resource to support students and show how much time is left for a certain task or activity.

- Use visual calendars to show what is happening when.

- Reinforce basic concepts such as the sequence of days, months and seasons whenever possible.

Attention and concentration

Children and young people with difficulties with attention and concentration, such as ADHD (attention deficit hyperactivity disorder) may have difficulty with: focusing for extended periods; sitting still; fidgeting; daydreaming; or completing tasks. This can mean that they do not always know what is going on in the classroom, which can often lead to them getting into trouble.

Top tips

- Provide visual or written checklists and task boards so that students have a visual reminder of what they have to do.

- Use timers to help students remain focused on a task for a set amount of time.

- Provide a stress ball or small item to fiddle with if this helps concentration.

- Teach students to identify when and how they need to seek clarification if their attention has wandered.

- Use a home–school book to ensure that important messages are passed on.

Social communication difficulties

Many students with speech and language difficulties or autism spectrum conditions (including Asperger's syndrome) will have difficulties with social communication (how we use language and communication appropriately according to the context and audience, and how we maintain social relationships). Other students may also need to be taught social communication rules explicitly as they may not have had the necessary role models when younger. Difficulties can include:

- having frequent 'falling outs' or arguments with friends

- being unable to make or maintain friendships

- difficulties 'keeping up' in conversation

- difficulties understanding figurative language and the unwritten rules of conversation

- being unsure of other people's intentions

- coming across as rude and aggressive, or as shy and withdrawn.

All of these difficulties may mean that students feel lonely, left out or isolated. They may lack a supportive group of friends with whom they can talk through problems and ask for advice. Others may find that they frequently get into trouble.

Top tips

- Some students may benefit from taking part in a social communication group to develop these skills in a small, supportive environment.

- Teach social rules explicitly and revisit them frequently.

- Use peer mentoring or 'break-time buddies' to support vulnerable students during social times.

- Support students to 'unpick' situations and to identify where the misunderstanding occurred.

- Teach students specific ways of seeking clarification and solving problems.

- Many students will find unstructured break and lunch times difficult. Providing some structured activities can support these students to make new friends.

Mild or moderate learning difficulties

Children and young people with a global learning difficulty will have language skills, friendship skills and learning skills all in line with their general development. This can distance them from their peer group and the gap may widen as they grow older. Students may have difficulties in all of the areas mentioned above.

Repeated educational failure

Students who have experienced repeated educational failure are likely to have low self-esteem and are more likely to have a negative opinion of school. They may be embarrassed by their failure and lack a supportive peer group. Some may try to avoid tasks, refuse to work or engage in low-level disruption in the classroom. Students may have a gloomy picture of their future.

Low self-esteem

Any of these difficulties can create a sense of low self-esteem. Students with low self-esteem may:

- withdraw from activities

- not join in activities they would enjoy

- lack confidence to participate

- not feel able to ask for help

- focus on their own weaknesses and mistakes

- blame themselves for what has gone wrong

- not have the confidence to try new things.

Over time, this can lead to frustration, depression and anxiety.

The theory and concepts underpinning this book

Mental health

So, what is meant by the term 'mental health'? The World Health Organization describes mental health as:

> **a state of well-being in which every individual realizes his or her own potential, can cope with the normal stresses of life, can work productively and fruitfully, and is able to make a contribution to her or his community. Health is a state of complete physical, mental and social well-being and not merely the absence of disease or infirmity.**

(WHO, 2014)

The European Commission also defines mental health as being more than simply the absence of mental illness, describing mental health as: 'a resource which enables them to realise their intellectual and emotional potential and to find and fulfil their roles in social, school and working life. For societies, good mental health of citizens contributes to prosperity, solidarity and social justice' (European Commission, 2005).

Positive psychology

Many of the ideas and activities in this book stem from the positive psychology movement. Psychology traditionally has focused on psychological deficits, diseases and disabilities, whereas positive psychology can be considered as the scientific study of human strengths and happiness which seeks to identify factors that can promote wellbeing. Positive psychology (a movement based on the work of Martin Seligman) aims to enhance wellbeing and happiness rather than remediate deficits. Similarly, this book seeks to promote mental wellbeing, rather than 'fix' something within individuals.

Initially, Seligman (2002) proposed three routes to happiness, out of which the field of positive psychology has grown.

- The pleasant life – being able to enjoy positive emotions and experiences.

- The engaged life – being able to use your strengths constructively (eg using and developing positive traits, developing emotional intelligence).

- The meaningful life – being part of something bigger than yourself (eg maintaining social responsibilities and connections, altruism).

The field of positive psychology encompasses some of the following areas.

Strengths and virtues	Emotional intelligence	Positive emotions
Positive coping strategies or resilience	Characteristics of positive individuals and groups	Self-esteem and self-efficacy
Flow	Happiness	Motivation
Creativity	Wellbeing	Positive therapy

This book aims to enable students with special educational needs to uncover their strengths and gain increasing self-awareness; skills that will help them to develop resilience and self-esteem. Ideas from the positive psychology movement have been used to develop many of the activities in Part 2.

Self-esteem

This resource also pays particular attention to developing self-esteem. Self-esteem can be defined as how we see ourselves, often in comparison with the ideal self we would like to be. The development of self-esteem begins in childhood and continues into adulthood. Our level of self-esteem is often a reflection of 'parental attitudes, opinions and behaviour, and school expectations, both academic and social' (McGirl, 2009, p10).

Low self-esteem can limit an individual's motivation and ability to enjoy, achieve and participate in all areas of everyday life. Self-esteem also includes our beliefs about our own worth and competence, and affects our attitude towards taking on challenges and new experiences. Low self-esteem is often associated with an increased risk of loneliness, resentment, depression, anxiety, irritability, eating disorders and negative risk-taking behaviours such as substance abuse (Jellineck *et al*, 2002).

Labels and diagnosis

Although certain groups of children and young people may benefit particularly from using this resource, it is not designed only for those with an identified special educational need or diagnosed condition. This resource takes a person-centred view, seeing the development of personal wellbeing as essential to all, regardless of their 'label' or 'condition'. Professor Peter Kinderman (2013) proposes the notion that 'our thoughts, our emotions, our behaviour and, therefore, our mental health are largely dependent on our understanding of the world, our thoughts about ourselves, other people, the future, and the world.' Kinderman continues that 'in this view of the world, of human nature, there is no real need to invoke the idea of abnormality or disease, even of diagnosis – people are just making sense of their world; developing complex, shifting, emotionally-laden frameworks of understanding of the world'.

This resource reflects the importance of enabling children and young people to make sense of their own world and sees every child and young person as having the potential to improve their sense of wellbeing, regardless of any 'label' they may have been given or feel limited by.

Benefits of using this approach

Mental wellbeing enables children to play and learn, to develop a sense of right and wrong and to make and maintain positive relationships. The benefits are summarised below.

Approach		Outcomes for child or young person
Developing a better idea of strengths, likes and dislikes	→	Increased self-esteem More likely to engage with enjoyable and productive activities More likely to choose a programme of study and job suited to their interests and skills Aids goal setting and motivation
Improving ability to identify, discuss and explore emotions and feelings	→	Better able to self-regulate and respond to situations positively Develop increased emotional intelligence Able to better identify feelings in others and therefore able to make and maintain friendships and social relationships
Developing ability to solve problems independently	→	Increased self-esteem and self-efficacy Improved behaviour in the classroom Feeling more empowered to confront challenges and try out new experiences
Developing ability to cultivate positive emotions and experiences	→	Helps to prevent worry and anxiety Builds a bank of positive memories Able to learn from setbacks and challenges

Further resources

The following websites provide more information about mental health.

- **www.youngminds.org.uk** – YoungMinds is the UK's leading charity committed to improving the emotional wellbeing and mental health of young people. The website contains sections for young people, parents and professionals.

- **www.mind.org.uk** – Mind offers advice and support for those experiencing mental health difficulties. The website contains advice on different types of mental health difficulty as well as information about services and training for professionals.

- **www.mentalhealth.org.uk** – a UK charity focusing on mental health research, policy and service improvement.

- **www.nhs.uk/livewell/mentalhealth** – information from the NHS on a range of conditions and services available.

- **www.b-eat.co.uk** – information about eating disorders and difficulties with food, weight and shape.

- **www.mentalhealth.org.uk** – the Mental Health Foundation website includes an A–Z of mental health topics and issues.

Training in various aspects of counselling and mental wellbeing is available at:

- **www.minded.org.uk** – MindEd offers over 250 e-learning modules and a wealth of information for anyone working with children or young people.

- **www.place2be.org.uk** – a national charity providing emotional support to children in schools. Place2Be also provides training and qualifications to those working with children and young people.

There is information for young people at:

- **www.youngminds.org.uk** – contains a section for young people about how to look after themselves and how mental health difficulties may affect them

- **www.headmeds.org.uk** – information and advice for young people taking medication for mental health conditions

- **www.thesite.org/mental-health** – information and advice for teenagers about a range of topics.

Further reading

Boniwell I (2008) *Positive Psychology in a Nutshell*, PWBC, London.

Carr A (2011) *Positive Psychology: The Science of Happiness and Human Strengths*, Routledge, London.

Seligman M (2002) *Authentic Happiness*, Free Press, New York.

Introduction for children and young people

Welcome to *The Sky's the Limit*. You may have been given this book to work through with a teacher, parent, carer, social worker or support worker in or out of school. This book will help you to learn about yourself. It will help you to discover your own likes and interests, find out what you are good at, and identify what makes you feel happy and sad. It will also help you to cope with any problems that come up. This book begins with a short story and then contains activities and games which you can complete either with an adult or with other young people in your group.

Growing up can be a difficult time. You have to cope with many new and difficult situations such as family, friendships, relationships, schoolwork, exams and having more independence. Sometimes these things can cause bigger problems.

Remember that if you have a problem, there are many people who can help you. It helps if you speak to somebody. You may want to start by speaking to an adult you can trust – maybe a parent or carer, or somebody who you can trust at school, such as a teacher or teaching assistant. Your school may also have a school nurse or a school counsellor who you can speak to. A counsellor is somebody you can speak to confidentially about your thoughts, feelings and behaviour. Confidentially means that they won't tell anybody what you say, unless someone is in danger.

You may also like to find more information at
www.youngminds.org.uk/for_children_young_people/

Part 1

The story

Introduction

This part of the book contains a story in which two characters – Sam and Ali – discuss the idea of mental wellbeing. Students will benefit from reading this story with an adult and using each page as the basis for a discussion. Students can then return to the story later, after having completed the activities, and link each page to their own experiences.

Meet Sam and Ali.

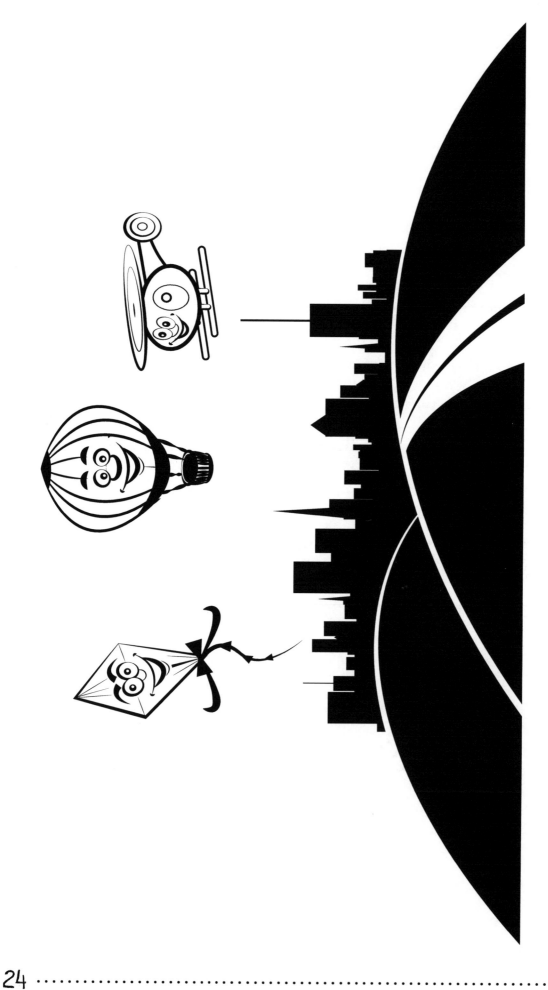

Sam and Ali enjoy doing different things, travelling to new places and meeting interesting people.

Speechmark

There are lots more things Sam and Ali would like to do in the future.

Today Ali is feeling confused.

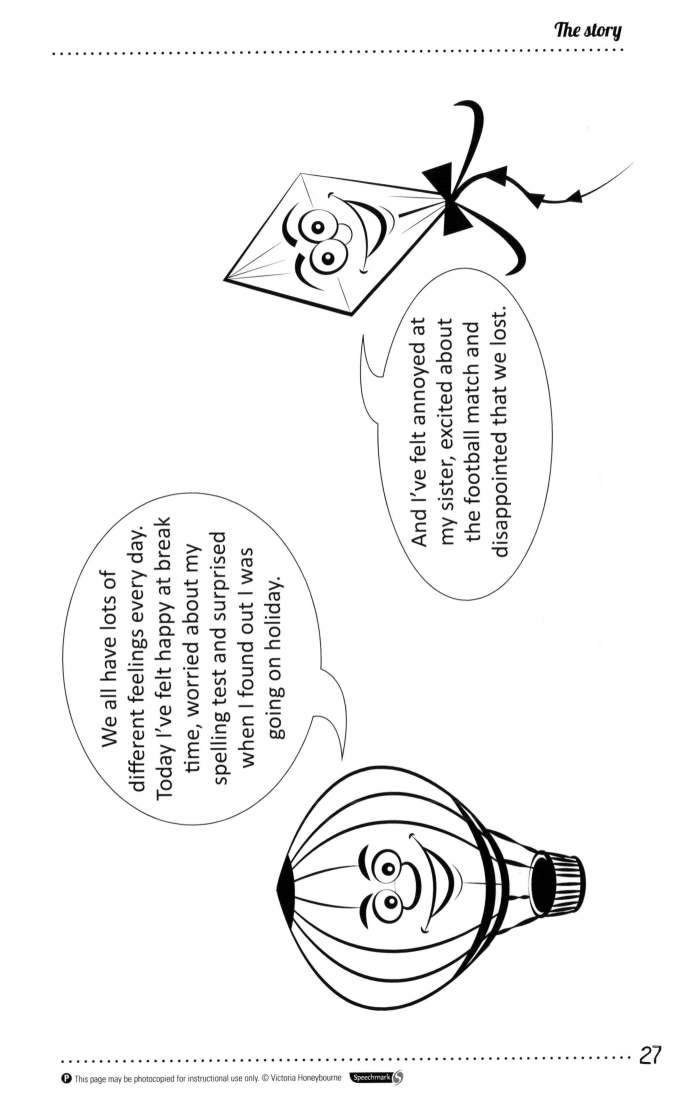

And I've felt annoyed at my sister, excited about the football match and disappointed that we lost.

We all have lots of different feelings every day. Today I've felt happy at break time, worried about my spelling test and surprised when I found out I was going on holiday.

Speechmark

Sometimes difficult things can happen which make us sad.

There are different types of problems. Some things can make us feel down for a short time. We can solve the problem and then feel better.

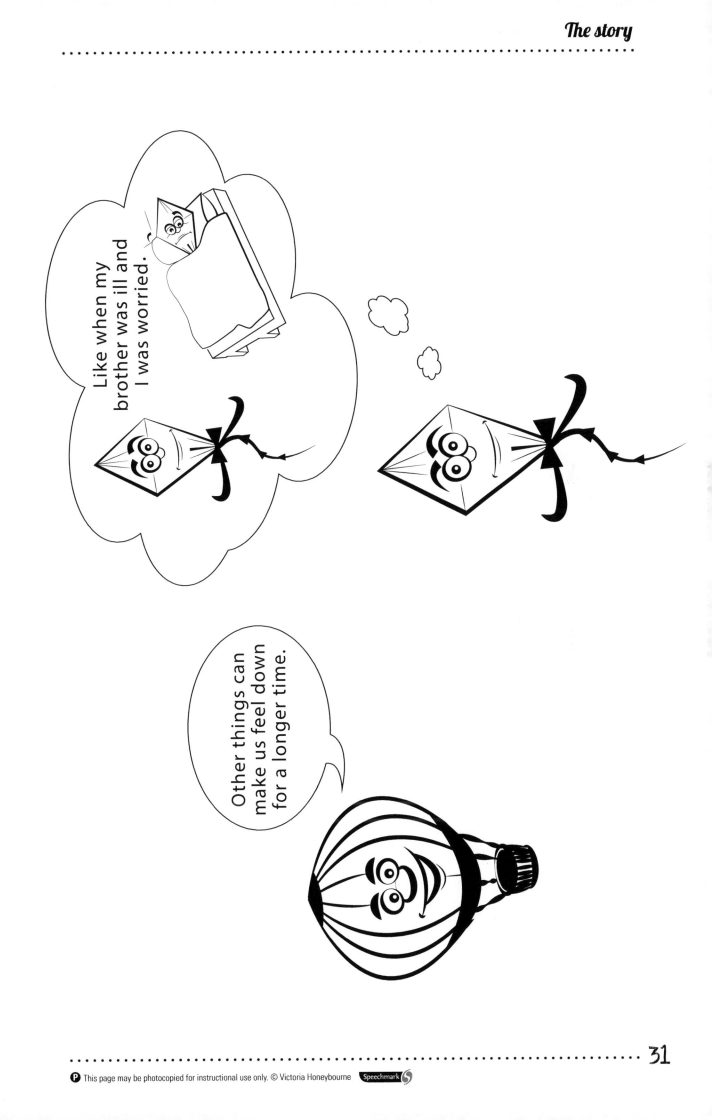

Speechmark ⑤

Speechmark Ⓢ

But other problems can start more slowly and over time we gradually don't feel so good.

Speechmark

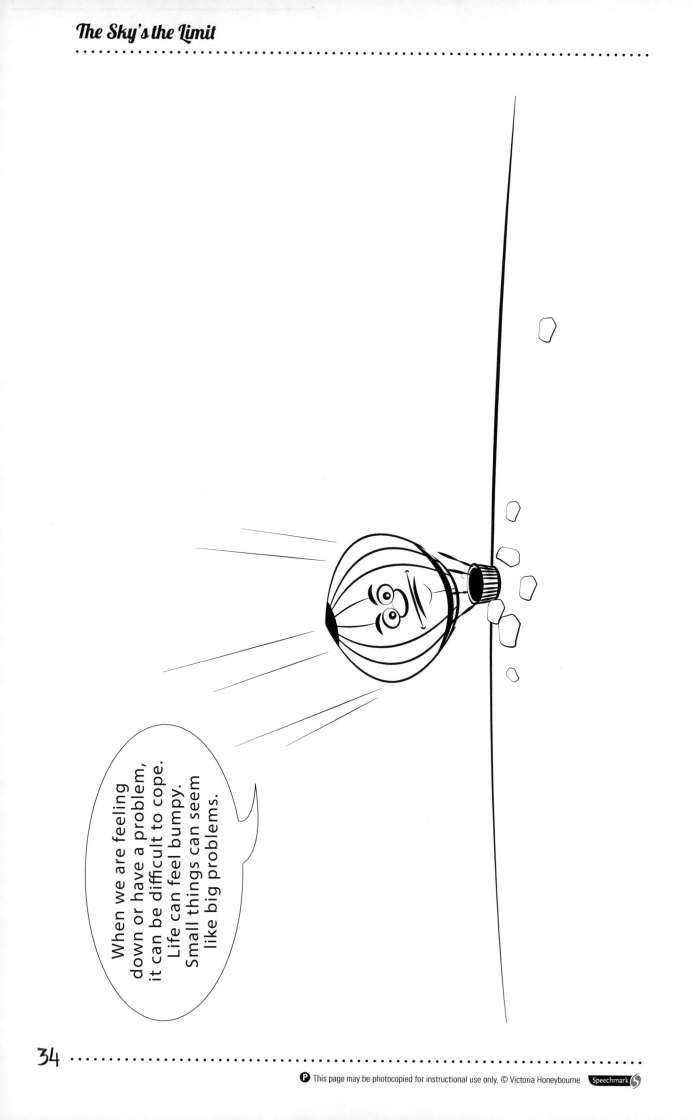

We might feel lonely, left out or isolated.

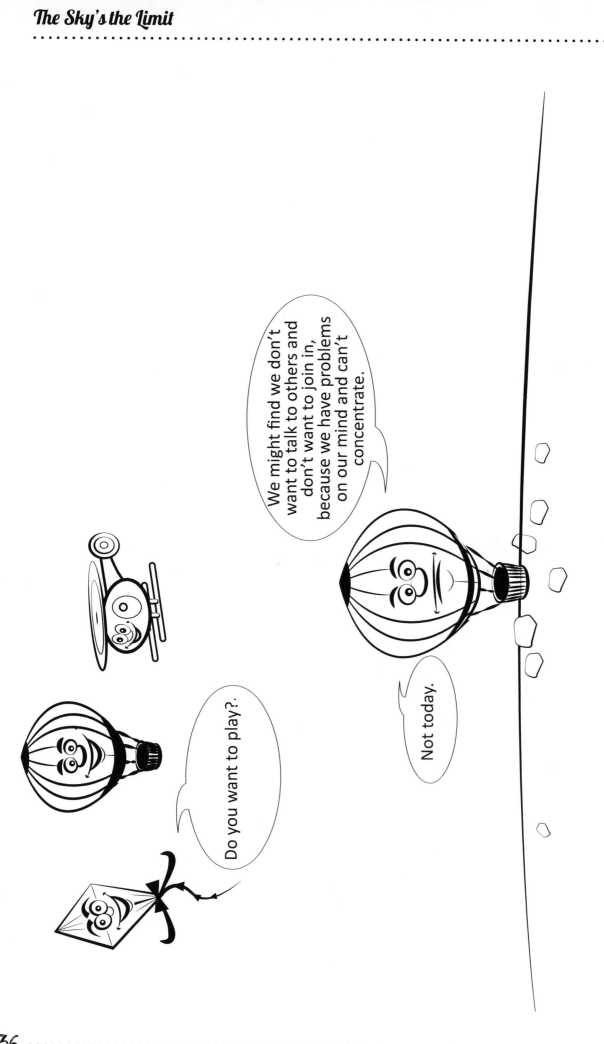

Speechmark

We might feel irritable, easily upset or depressed.

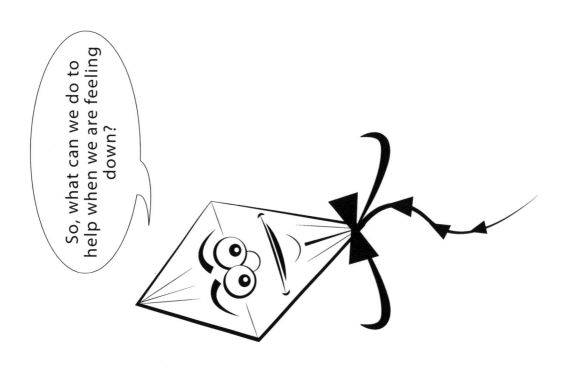

Speechmark

Speechmark Ⓢ

I am good at asking questions and talking to people, so if I had a problem, I could talk to others to see if they could give me some ideas.

We can use our strengths to help us solve problems

Speechmark

Sometimes it can help to do some breathing or relaxation exercises.

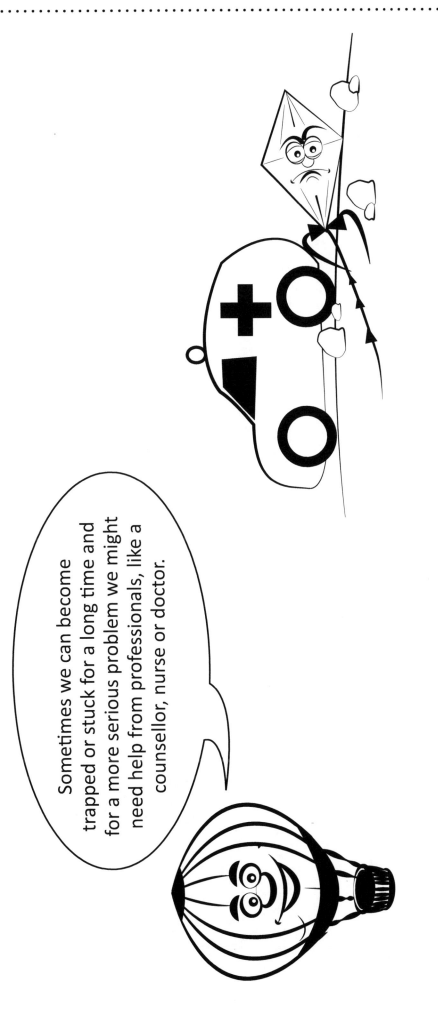

Sometimes we can become trapped or stuck for a long time and for a more serious problem we might need help from professionals, like a counsellor, nurse or doctor.

But there are lots of things we can do to help us cope with these things.

There are lots of good things to look forward to, but we will also sometimes come across problems and not feel so good.

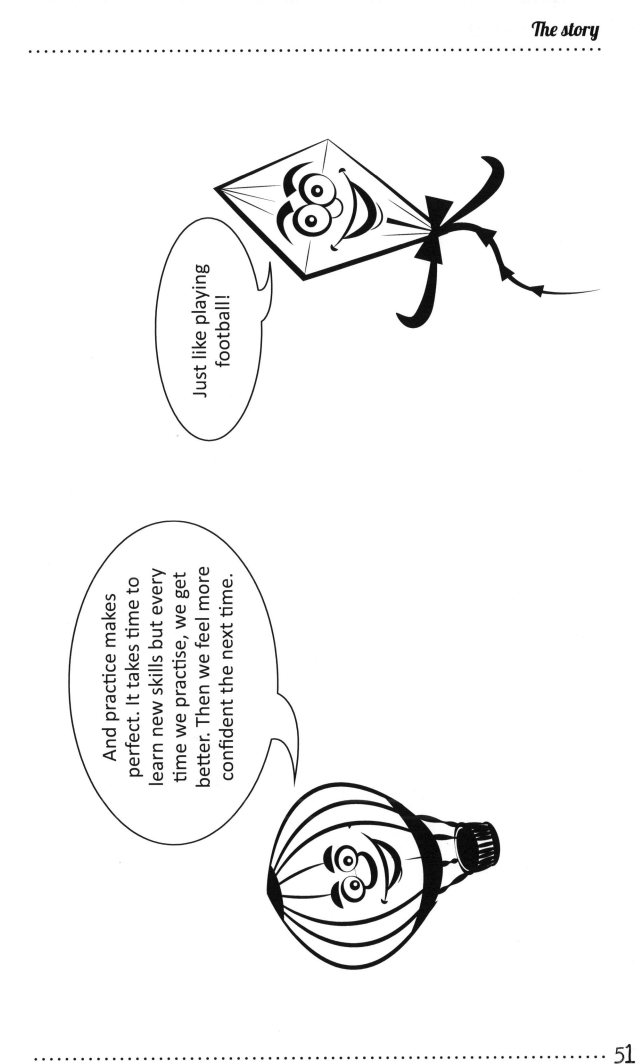

Speechmark

Part 2
The activities

Introduction

This part of the resource contains the activities and their associated worksheets. The activities are grouped as follows.

- Ground rules

- Who am I?

- Past, present and future

- Keeping healthy

- My emotions and feelings

- Getting on with other people

- Using the positives

Each activity begins with 'Teaching notes' which outline the ways of delivering and differentiating the activities. The worksheet provided for each activity can be copied and given to each student. Further background information for adults is included in 'Good to know' boxes and there are ideas for adapting some of the activities for whole-class use in 'Whole-school idea' boxes.

It is recommended that the activities are delivered in the order they are provided, as some of the later tasks build on information and skills gained earlier. However, not all of the activities will be relevant to all children and young people, so adults should use their professional judgement when deciding which tasks to present.

Most of the activities are designed to be ongoing rather than stand alone. Mental wellbeing is a continuous process which pervades every aspect of everyday life, rather than something that can be taught and assimilated in discrete sessions. Students will develop their understanding of themselves and others over time, and therefore will benefit from continuing with, or revisiting, some of the activities over time (eg keep adding to their list of achievements, continue using problem-solving techniques). It can, therefore, be useful if students keep their worksheets and notes together in a folder, to refer back to and to support them in applying the skills learned to everyday situations.

Materials or equipment required

No specific equipment is required to deliver the activities. Most of them can be completed with paper and coloured pencils. However, some students may benefit from using computers, cameras or other software they are comfortable with.

Ground rules

If this intervention is being delivered in a small group, or indeed with individuals, it can be appropriate to begin the sessions with some 'ground rules'. This sets the tone of the group and helps to prevent future misunderstandings or worries.

Activity 1 Ground rules

Teaching notes

1. Begin by ensuring that students know where, when and how often the group sessions will take place. It is also important to explain to students why they are taking part in the group. A good starting point is to explain to students that this group will help them to learn more about what they are good at, their feelings and how they can solve any problems that arise. You could also read the 'Introduction for children and young people' at the beginning of this book.

2. Explain how every activity needs some rules (eg a game of football needs an equal number of players in the teams; otherwise one side has an advantage). Discuss with students what would happen if some rules were broken or if one team did not know what the rules were.

3. Ask students to generate some 'rules' or 'expectations' for this group. They could write these down, draw them, act them out or dictate them to an adult.

4. Here are some prompts if students struggle to generate ideas.

   • We will remain silent when other people are talking.

   • We will ask if we don't understand something.

   • We will respect what other people say.

   • We will not tell others outside the group what people say in here – it is confidential.

   • We will all try to take part as much as we can.

5. End by drawing up an agreed list of 'rules' or 'expectations' (see the next page).

Good to know
Some students will need these ground rules repeating frequently in order to remember them. It is best to do this at the beginning of each session. You could try displaying these 'rules' visibly during each session so that they can be referred to easily. For example: Joe, *do you remember we agreed that we would all wait until somebody has finished speaking before we gave our own opinion?*

Activity 1 'Ground rules' worksheet

Our group has agreed ...

1

2

3

4

5

6

Agreed by:

Date:

Activity 2 Introductions

Teaching notes

Some students with special educational needs will find it difficult to remember the names of both staff and their classmates. This can cause confusion or embarrassment, as well as make communication more difficult. (Have you ever tried to get somebody's attention when you didn't know their name? Did it make the task more difficult?) Names can be particularly problematic in secondary schools when students may come into contact with many different teachers, teaching assistants and support staff during a week.

It can be a good idea to create a visual resource which includes photographs of the people in the group (see the next page). Remember to introduce yourself too, and give students plenty of time to practise saying names, especially if they are long or unusual. If students don't know each other already, it can be a good idea to reintroduce everybody at the beginning of the first few sessions. Again, the poster created in this activity can be displayed during each session or a copy can be put at the front of each pupil's folder.

Good to know

Modelling social skills and emotional intelligence throughout these sessions can be one of the most effective ways of teaching these skills to students. You can do this by:

- Asking questions and seeking clarification if you don't understand what a pupil has said.
- Apologising if you make a mistake or forget something and showing students how you can rectify the situation effectively.
- Modelling the skills you expect of students (eg not interrupting, using 'please' and 'thank you').

Whole-school idea

It can be helpful for all students if staff names and photographs are displayed on classroom doors or wall displays. Remember also to include learning support assistants, lunch-time staff and pastoral staff.

Activity 2 'Introductions' worksheet

The people in our group are:

Who am I?

Once ground rules and introductions have been completed, the next set of activities focuses on developing a sense of self, discovering that no two people are exactly the same, and identifying strengths, skills and talents.

Activity 3 My favourites

Teaching notes

This activity can be completed in several ways, depending on the interests and abilities of the students involved. Students fill in each bubble on the worksheet on the next page with either pictures or words about their favourite things. Some students may want to write, others may prefer to draw, create a collage of photographs, use a computer, or make a slideshow, a video or an animation. Students can also add their own categories of 'favourites' to make a poster.

Follow-up discussion

This activity can be a good starting point to enable students to talk about themselves using quite neutral and non-threatening topics. Students may like to present their completed poster to the rest of the group or talk in more detail about some of the things they have identified. It can be beneficial at this point to discuss how we all like different things and the importance of respecting other people's opinions, even if they are different from our own.

Activity 3 'My favourites' worksheet

This is me: ——————————————

My favourite …

Colour:

Food:

Lesson:

Sport:

Hobby:

Television show:

Book or music:

Activity 4 Likes and dislikes

Teaching notes

This is similar to the previous activity but designed to be less restrictive and to help students to reflect on their likes and dislikes in more detail. Students can include more abstract ideas (eg 'people who are mean', 'being teased') as well as more concrete ones (eg 'maths', 'spiders', 'peas').

Follow-up discussion

Ensure that students realise that we all have different likes and dislikes – there are no right or wrong answers. Some students will find this task easier if given prompts of various categories that they can choose likes and dislikes from, for example:

school subjects	sports	hobbies	food/drink
places	types of people	animals	events
times of year	times of day	days of week	experiences
television / computer games / books / music			rules

Again, students can either fill in the worksheet provided or use their preferred method to record and present this activity.

Good to know: open and closed questions

Closed questions are those which require a 'yes' or 'no' answer, or factual information (*Do you like football? How old are you?*).

Open questions allow the speaker to share their opinions more fully and give an extended answer (*What did you think of the school trip yesterday? How did you feel?*).

Leading questions ask somebody to agree with a suggestion (*Do you think maths is boring? Wouldn't it be better if you went to the party?*).

Leading questions should be avoided when trying to allow children and young people to express themselves authentically. Closed questions can be useful for establishing facts but open questions are best to use to find out about behaviour, beliefs and feelings (MindEd, 2015).

Be careful of overusing 'why'. For many people, too many 'Why?' questions can sound intrusive and interrogatory (*Why did you do that? Why didn't you go home?*) (Leimon & McMahon, 2009).

Activity 4 'Likes and dislikes' worksheet

This is me: _____

Things I like:

Things I dislike:

Speechmark

Activity 5   Things others like and admire about me

Teaching notes

This activity is designed for students to discover what other people like and admire about them. This can create a starting point to support students in identifying their strengths and skills. Students should try to ask a range of people outside the group to fill in a speech bubble about them and write their own name underneath. They may choose to ask friends, classmates, parents or carers, school staff, siblings, family members, or activity leaders. People contributing to this activity should be asked to consider personal characteristics and skills as well as talents.

Here is an example:

You are very kind to others – you help them to join in games.

By Miss Smith

You always try your best with things.

By Amy

Discussion

- How did students feel about doing this activity?
- Were they surprised at anything people said?
- Can they think of specific examples of when they have displayed these skills?

Whole-school idea

This activity can also be helpful for students who are preparing their pupil profiles or preparing for their Education, Health and Care Plan (EHCP) review meetings.

Activity 5 'What others like and admire about me' worksheet

This is me: _____

Activity 6 Skills, strengths and talents

Teaching notes

Whereas some students will be able to identify their strengths and skills relatively easily, others may have difficulty recognising and naming them.

> **Good to know**
> Research shows that top achievers build both their personal lives and careers on their talents and strengths by finding roles which suit them best and applying their strengths and talents to various situations and experiences (Boniwell, 2008).

Activity 6a provides lists of things students may be good at, with empty boxes for students to add their own. Students can highlight the skills that apply to them or use this page as a cut-and-stick activity to create their own 'skills' poster.

Some students will then be able to move on to the match-up exercise in Activity 6b. Some personal characteristics are listed to match to the definitions. These terms may be new to some students, so the vocabulary may need additional teaching. See Appendix 1 for tips on teaching new vocabulary.

Many young people with special educational needs or communication needs can find it difficult to learn and remember new vocabulary. When introducing vocabulary relating to feelings, emotions or personal characteristics, you might like to use some of the vocabulary resources included in Appendix 1.

Discussion

- Once students have identified their skills and strengths, can they think of specific examples when they have shown these?
- Are there any famous people or celebrities they know who display these characteristics?
- Are there any traits on the list they would like to develop further?

Answers for Activity 6b

You are original and find new ways of doing things	**creative** **optimistic**	You are hopeful and look for positive things
You are thankful for all the good things that happen	**perseverance** **gratitude**	You keep on trying even though things are difficult
You do things with energy and enthusiasm	**enthusiasm** **self-control**	You control your thinking and behaviour when it is necessary
You look after and help other people	**open-minded** **kindness**	You respect other people's opinions and consider them
You can be trusted and know the difference between right and wrong	**responsible** **forgiving**	You can forgive people and give them a second chance
You can direct and organise activities and encourage others to join in	**reliable** **leadership**	You can be trusted to do what you say you will do
You tell the truth	**honest** **fairness**	You give everybody a fair chance, regardless of your personal opinions
You get on well with others in social situations	**curiosity** **sociable**	You are interested in new things and ask questions

Activity 6a 'Skills, strengths and talents' worksheet

Things I am good at

School subjects

Maths	Writing	Reading	Science
Art	Music	Drama	PE
Languages	History	Geography	Religious studies
Design technology	Personal, Social, Health and Economic education (PSHE)	Computing	

Hobbies and interests

Drawing	Making things	Lego®	Reading
Computers	Board games	Card games	Football
Tennis	Gymnastics	Dance	Martial arts
Swimming	Running	Musical instrument	Brownies / Cubs / Guides / Scouts
Baking			

Skills

Looking after animals	Helping others	Keeping things tidy
Listening to others	Answering in class	Working with others
Working by myself	Getting homework done	Looking after plants
Building things	Following instructions	Asking for help
Helping others join in	Solving problems	Trying my best
Learning new things	Remembering things	

Activity 6b 'Personal characteristics' worksheet

Match the words in the middle with the correct definition from the left-hand or right-hand column. Which words describe you?

You are original and find new ways of doing things	**creative** **optimistic**	You are hopeful and look for positive things
You are thankful for all the good things that happen	**perseverance** **gratitude**	You keep on trying even though things are difficult
You do things with energy and enthusiasm	**enthusiasm** **self-control**	You control your thinking and behaviour when it is necessary
You look after and help other people	**open-minded** **kindness**	You respect other people's opinions and consider them
You can be trusted and know the difference between right and wrong	**responsible** **forgiving**	You can forgive people and give them a second chance
You can direct and organise activities and encourage others to join in	**reliable** **leadership**	You can be trusted to do what you say you will do
You tell the truth	**honest** **fairness**	You give everybody a fair chance, regardless of your personal opinions
You get on well with others in social situations	**curiosity** **sociable**	You are interested in new things and ask questions

Activity 7 All about me

Teaching notes

This activity is designed for students to bring together everything they have learned so far to create an 'All about me' profile. Again, there are different ways for students to present this other than filling in the worksheet provided. For example, they can use writing, drawings, collage, video, animation or computers.

Some students may also like to use this as their 'student profile' to share with the adults who support them in and out of school.

Whole-school idea

All students in a year group could complete this activity at the beginning of a school year to help staff get to know them.

Activity 7 'All about me' worksheet

Photo:	Name:
	Age:

Things I like:

Things I am good at:

My skills and strengths:

How other people describe me:

Things that help me to learn:

Things that I find difficult:

Past, present and future

Teaching notes

The next group of activities considers what students have done well in the past and looks to the future. By thinking back, students can be supported to identify past achievements and successes and, in looking to the future, students can begin to identify what is important to them and the goals they would like to aim for.

Activity 8   My past achievements

Teaching notes

The timeline on the next page can be filled in with years or ages and students can then add the achievements they are most proud of. These can come from any area of their lives. They may include things such as 'I learned how to swim', 'I passed my music exam', 'I learned how to ride a bike', 'I began to walk to school by myself'.

This activity is presented as a timeline to support students with time concepts and the idea of sequencing. Again, photographs or drawings may be more appropriate for some students.

Discussion

- Ask students why they are most proud of certain achievements.

- How did they learn new things?

- What was difficult at the time and how did they overcome this?

There is a completed example on the next page.

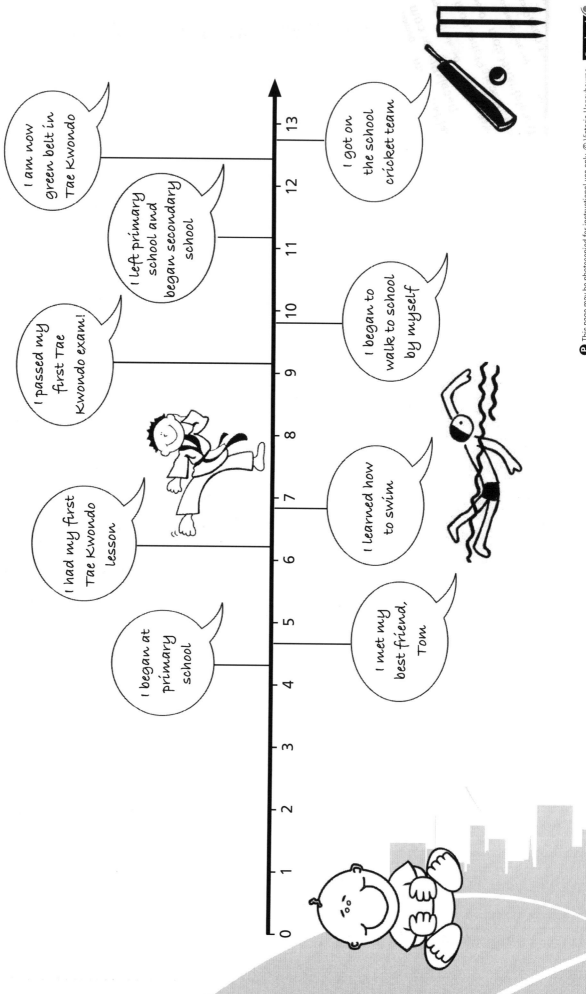

Speechmark

Activity 8 'My past achievements' timeline

Activity 9 My achievements

Teaching notes

Achievements can be big or small and can happen on a daily basis. This activity builds on the previous one by asking students to consider what they are doing well at the present time. This activity can work particularly well if students add to their posters regularly over an extended period of time.

You may like to create a larger poster for each pupil based on the chart on the next page. New achievements can then be added, in words, pictures or on sticky notes. This can build up into a powerful visual reminder of what students are doing well. Achievements could include things like:

- 'I finished the blue level of reading books'

- 'I forgot my homework but explained this to my teacher politely'

- 'I won a class award'

- 'I produced a neater piece of work'

- 'I didn't understand the science homework, so I went to homework club at lunchtime'.

Idea

Ensure that all adults working with students know that they are keeping an achievement chart. Other staff can also point out to students what they are doing well at different times during the school day. Parents and carers can also be asked to tell students explicitly when they have done something well and these can also be added to their chart.

Here is a completed example:

Whole-school idea

Students could have an 'achievements' page in their planners or home–school books to record the positive achievements that are happening every day.

Activity 9 'My achievements' chart

My achievements

Activity 10 My memory wall

Teaching notes

This activity is designed for students to keep a record of happy memories. Rather than use the worksheet provided, students may prefer to keep a scrapbook, use an online scrapbook or create a slideshow or video.

Some prompts of experiences that students may like to include are:

- times spent with family or friends
- pets
- holidays
- school trips
- special events
- hobbies
- favourite things.

Discussion

Ask students why these memories are special to them. Research shows that positive reminiscence can help us to hold on to memories of good times and intensify these experiences.

Whole-school idea
All students could add special memories in the form of photographs, drawings, writing or mementos to a 'yearbook' which they can continue adding to during their school career. They will then leave with a concrete reminder of positive memories and achievements.

Activity 10 'My memory wall' worksheet

My memories ...

Speechmark Ⓢ

Activity 11 My wishes for the future

Teaching notes

Facing the future eagerly and hopefully is key to developing real happiness (Leimon & McMahon, 2009). Consider the difference in mindset of someone who is facing the future with fear and dread from someone who hopes their life is going to be full of good experiences, interesting people and new friends. Our attitude to the future can affect our present motivation, confidence and wellbeing.

Encourage students to be creative in completing the worksheet for this activity and to think about all areas of their life. What is important to them? For example:

- Learning how to drive a car?

- Having friends?

- Getting a job?

- Pursuing a hobby?

- Travelling?

- Good health?

- Getting a pet?

- Going to college?

Discussion

Why have students chosen these things? Encourage students to think about what is important to them and create an image of their future. Remember the future can be both short term (what to do in the upcoming half-term) and long term (future career aspirations).

Activities 12 and 13 then go on to support students to sequence their ideas and set more concrete goals.

Activity 11 'My future wishes' worksheet

My future wishes are ...

Speechmark Ⓢ

Activity 12 My future

Teaching notes

This activity is designed to help students think about their future and gain a better understanding of what will happen when. Again, this is designed as a timeline in order to support those students who have difficulty with time concepts and dates.

Start by labelling the timeline on the next page with years or ages, depending on which is easier for the pupil to understand. Students can then add in important events (eg exams, leaving school, being old enough to drive a car, getting a job) and their wishes for the future at appropriate points (eg 'I would like to live with friends', 'I would like to go on holiday to the USA').

Discussion

- Are students worried about anything on their timeline?

- Do they need to find out more information about anything?

- What would they like more help with?

There is a completed example on the next page.

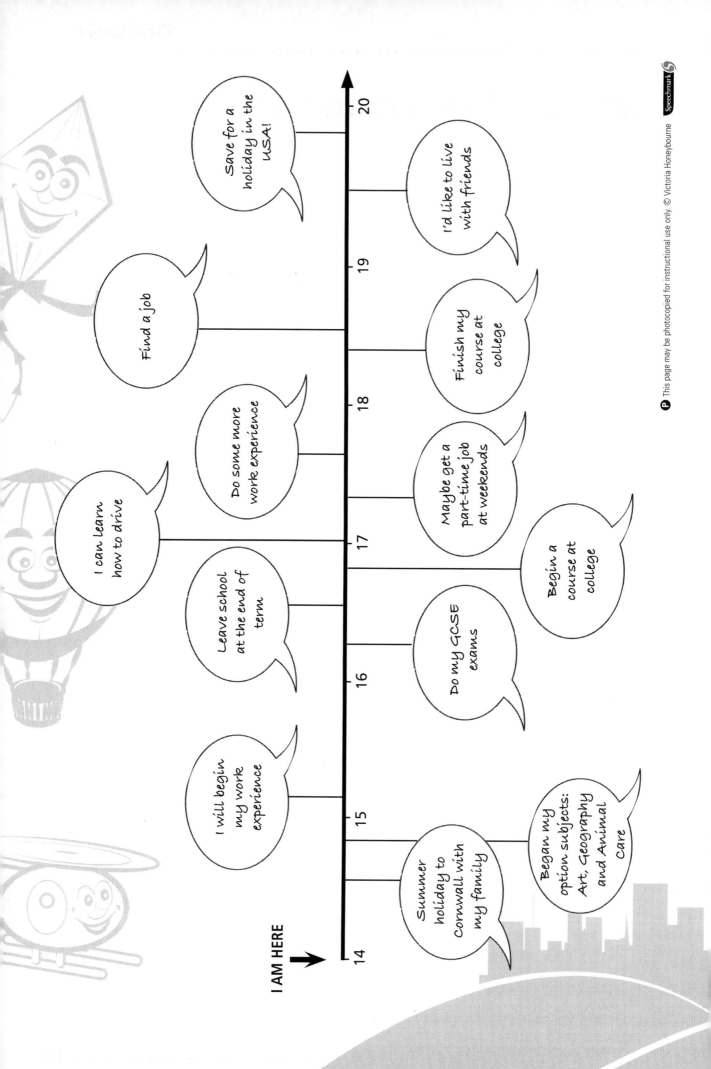

I AM HERE

Activity 12 'My future' timeline

Activity 13 Goal setting

Teaching notes

This activity is linked directly to the previous one and focuses on goal-setting techniques. Once students have identified their wishes for the future, it is then important to feel they are actively working towards these goals and to know what they need to do next. This activity provides a template of how to set goals and a checklist. You may like to photocopy the sheet on the next page for students to use for different goals.

Here is a completed example:

What is your goal?
I am in a singing group and would like to arrange a visit to an old people's home to sing them some Christmas songs.

What smaller steps will lead to this goal?	When does this step have to be done?	Who can help you with this step?	Tick when done
1 Ask my music teacher to help me phone the old people's home to arrange a good time and day to visit.	This week	Mrs Smith	✓
2 Tell the others in the singing group and make sure they can all attend.	This week	The other singers	✓
3 Decide as a group which songs we will sing and in which order.	By 1st December	The other singers	✓
4 Rehearse these songs.	Singing club every week before Christmas.	The other singers and Mrs Smith	✓
5 Find some Santa hats for us all to wear.	By 20th December	My sister who had one last year	✓
6 Bake some Christmas cupcakes to take with us for the old people.	The day before – 21st December.	Mum and the other singers	✓

What problems could you face on the way?	How could you solve these problems?
We might not be able to decide on the songs or might not be able to make the same day. Some people might be ill on the day.	We can discuss together which songs to sing and which day will be best. We can all practise the songs so if somebody is ill and can't make it, then it won't be a problem.

Reflection: What went well?
We were very well rehearsed, we had found Santa hats, the cupcakes were good and the old people really enjoyed it.

What would you do differently next time?
There were more people than we thought so we hadn't baked enough cupcakes. We also forgot our speakers. Next time we need to ask how many people will be there and make a list of who will take the equipment.

Activity 13 'Goal setting' checklist

What is your goal			
What smaller steps will lead to this goal?	**When does this step have to be done?**	**Who can help you with this step?**	**Tick when done**
1			
2			
3			
4			
5			
6			

What problems could you face on the way?.	How could you solve these problems?

Reflection:
What went well?

What would you do differently next time?

Keeping healthy

'A healthy mind in a healthy body' is an age-old saying but there is plenty of recent evidence which suggests that keeping physically healthy by eating well, exercising and getting enough rest helps mental wellbeing. Doing physical exercise in particular has been shown to improve mood and be uplifting.

Whole-School ideas

Keeping physically healthy helps to promote mental wellbeing as well as leading to many health benefits. Schools and other settings can help to support physical wellbeing in several ways.

- Ensure that a range of sports and games are offered in PE lessons to suit all interests. Some students with communication difficulties or low self-esteem may find team games particularly difficult or intimidating and may prefer to engage in individual sports such as trampolining, aerobics, dance or swimming.

- Provide a range of active options for extra-curricular activities at break and lunch times and after school. Organised and supervised outdoor games and activities can be a healthier alternative to lunch time computer clubs.

- Link up with local leisure providers to ensure that students and parents are aware of the activities available in their local community. More unusual sports such as martial arts or Zumba classes can be popular options for young people who would not necessarily see themselves as 'sporty'.

- Encourage students and parents or carers to walk or cycle to school rather than taking the car.

- Ensure that a range of healthy food options are on offer at break and lunch times in the school canteen.

- Teach children and young people how to cook and prepare healthy meals and snacks.

- Involve parents and carers in the school's work on healthy lifestyles. The school nurse may be able to direct families to appropriate support with healthy eating and sleep hygiene.

Yawn!

Did you know that a lack of sleep can lead to irritability and a lack of focus and concentration, as well as tiredness and fatigue? Long-term lack of sleep can also lead to depression and anxiety, as well as increasing the risk of heart disease, diabetes and obesity (NHS, 2013).

Research suggests that a lack of sleep in young people can lead to poor performance in school which can have a negative effect on memory, concentration and behaviour (NHS, 2013).

Activity 14 Health and fitness

Teaching notes

The activity for this section is a point-scoring game which can be played by either individuals or teams. Students tend to get very excited about this game because the allocation of points is completely random and it is not necessarily the team that gives most correct answers that wins. It is also an effective way of reinforcing some basic maths skills.

How to play

1. Photocopy the true or false statements on page 90 on coloured paper and cut out to make cards.

2. Photocopy the scoring cards on a different colour paper, cut into cards and place them in a small bag or box.

3. Students or teams take it in turns to pick a question card. The game works best with two to four players or teams. Players decide if the statement on the card is true or false and give a reason for their answer. If they answer correctly, they can pick out a scoring card at random.

4. These points are added or subtracted from their team's score (each team starts with zero). It helps to keep score on a whiteboard or piece of paper.

5. When all of the question cards have been used, the team with the most points wins the game.

Answers

The statements in this activity are intended to spark discussion of the issues in question. Some suggestions are given on the next page, but some students may benefit from more in-depth discussion or work on particular themes.

Young people between the ages of 5 and 18 should aim to be active for at least one hour every day. TRUE	Playing in the playground, skipping, walking the dog and cycling are good ways of keeping active. TRUE – these all count as moderately intense activity and are just as good for you as organised sports.
Spending a lot of time sitting in front of the television or computer is bad for you. TRUE	Swimming, rugby, football, trampolining, running, tennis, dancing and martial arts are all good for you. TRUE – any of these activities will benefit your health and you are more likely to stick with activities you enjoy.
Gymnastics, hopscotch, jumping, running and basketball all help to strengthen your bones. TRUE	Being active for at least an hour a day helps to keep your bones strong, your heart healthy and to keep you a healthy weight. TRUE – other benefits of exercise are also to promote self-confidence and can improve mood and social skills.
It is best to get the car to school. FALSE – walking or cycling are healthier options if possible.	You should do an hour of exercise all in one go. FALSE – you can do short amounts of activity throughout the day for the same benefits.
Fizzy drinks are bad for you. TRUE – they contain a lot of sugar so should only be drunk occasionally.	You should eat one fruit or vegetable every day. FALSE – it is recommended we eat at least five portions of fruit or vegetable every day.
Sleep helps us to keep healthy. TRUE – sleep helps us to concentrate, focus, feel happier and gives our body and brain time to repair and rest.	Four hours of sleep a night is not enough. TRUE – the average nine-year-old needs about 10 hours of sleep every night and a 14–16-year-old should aim for nine hours.
Having a warm bath, doing some relaxation exercises, or reading a book can help you to fall asleep. TRUE	Too many sweets, chocolate and crisps are bad for you. TRUE – these should be eaten in moderation.
Smoking is bad for your health. TRUE – smoking can lead to lung and breathing problems.	It is OK to skip breakfast. FALSE – eating a good breakfast gives us the energy we need for the morning.

Activity 14 Health and fitness 'true or false' cards

Young people between the ages of 5 and 18 should aim to be active for at least one hour every day.	Playing in the playground, skipping, walking the dog and cycling are good ways of keeping active.
Spending a lot of time sitting in front of the television or computer is bad for you.	Swimming, rugby, football, trampolining, running, tennis, dancing and martial arts are all good for you.
Gymnastics, hopscotch, jumping, running and basketball all help to strengthen your bones.	Being active for at least an hour a day helps to keep your bones strong, your heart healthy and to keep you a healthy weight.
It is best to get the car to school.	You should do an hour of exercise all in one go.
Fizzy drinks are bad for you.	You should eat one fruit or vegetable every day.
Sleep helps us to keep healthy	Four hours of sleep a night is not enough.
Having a warm bath, doing some relaxation exercises, or reading a book can help you to fall asleep.	Too many sweets, chocolate and crisps are bad for you.
Smoking is bad for your health.	It is OK to skip breakfast.

Activity 14 'Health and fitness' scoring cards

Add 5	Add 10	Add the number of days in a week	Add the number of months in a year
Subtract 10	Add the number of days in a year	Subtract 5	Add 50
Subtract 50	Double your points	Halve your points	Give half of your points to the team on your left
Add 25	Add your shoe size	Add your house number	Subtract 25
Give 20 of your points to the team on your right	Multiply your points by 2	Add the number of centimetres in a metre	Divide your points by 3
Multiply your points by 10	Add 40	Add 3	Add your age
Add the number of hours in a day	Add the number of minutes in an hour	Subtract the number of seconds in a minute	Add 100
Add your age times 5	Add your phone number	Triple your points	Add 47
Add 20	Add 500	Subtract 50	Give half of your points to the team on your right
Take another 2 cards	Divide by 2	Double your points	Miss a go

My emotions and feelings

By now, students have had the opportunity to identify their skills and strengths, consider their past and future, and discuss ways of keeping physically healthy. The next set of activities investigates emotions and feelings, helping students to express themselves and their worries.

Good to know: active listening

When children and young people are talking, one of the most important things adults can do is ensure that they feel truly listened to and accepted. 'Active listening' involves giving a speaker the opportunity to talk and reflect on their emotions without feeling judged or misunderstood. It is a term often used in counselling and talking therapies and can be a very powerful tool.

You can demonstrate active listening by:

- Showing you are listening through your own body language, facial expression, posture and gestures.

- Paying attention to what is said by avoiding environmental distractions and distracting thoughts.

- Asking questions to clarify certain points.

- Accepting what is said without commenting, judging or criticising.

- Reflecting back what the speaker is saying or summarising the main points every now and again.

(Source: adapted from McGirl, 2009)

Activity 15 Happy days

Teaching notes

This activity is designed to help students to identify what helps them to feel happy, an emotion which most children and young people will already be able to identify. Martin Seligman, who is regarded as one of the founders of modern positive psychology, suggests that encouraging the things that make us happy is one of the first steps in working towards the 'happy life' (Atkinson & Tomley, 2011).

Encourage the students to imagine what would be a happy day for them. For example:

- What activities would they do?

- Who would they spend the day with?

- Where would they go?

The results of the activity are presented as a diary to support the development of time concepts (see the next page). However, some students may prefer to write a story, or create a video or cartoon strip of their 'ideal day'.

Discussion

Asking students to present their 'happy day' will give a good insight into what helps them to feel happy, relaxed and comfortable. For example, is it doing certain hobbies, spending time with animals, being with friends and family? How could students be supported in doing more of the things that make them happy?

Activity 15 'Happy days' diary

A very happy day for me would look like this ...

Speechmark

Activity 16 What's that feeling?

Teaching notes

This activity encourages students to widen their vocabulary for emotions and feelings. The psychologist Paul Ekman (2003) proposed that there are seven universal basic emotions: anger, fear, disgust, contempt, happiness, sadness and surprise. However, there are many more feelings, and combinations of feelings, that we all experience.

'Explain feelings to the alien' game

This is a game for two to four players. A dice and small coloured counters are required to play. The playing board on the next page can be photocopied on card and enlarged. Students begin on the 'start' square and take it in turns to roll the dice, moving the required number of spaces. Students then have to explain to the alien, who does not know about human feelings, what is meant by the word on their square. (For example, *Surprised. You might feel surprised if somebody gave you a present that you weren't expecting.*) The first player to reach the 'finish' square wins.

Discussion

This game can be used as a basis for further discussion.

- When have students in the group experienced the emotion in question?

- How did it feel?

- How did they behave?

See Appendix 1 for some ideas on teaching new vocabulary.

> ### Good to know: right and wrong feelings?
> When discussing feelings, it is important that children and young people do not feel that there are 'right' and 'wrong' feelings. Accepting that it is OK to experience more negative feelings such as anger or frustration can be the first step in beginning to be able to cope effectively with these feelings.

Activity 16 'what's that feeling?' playing board

START	happy	sad	afraid	surprised	↘
↓	shocked	disgusted	excited	angry	nervous
worried	guilty	bored	disappointed	relieved	↘
↓	lonely	pleased	jealous	sorry	hurt
hopeful	annoyed	frustrated	upset	proud	↘
FINISH	embarrassed	enthusiastic	grumpy	cheerful	uncomfortable

I'm new to Earth and learning about human feelings

96

Speechmark

Activity 17 Big or little problem?

Teaching notes

All sorts of problems can make children and young people experience all sorts of feelings, some of which may cause worry or upset. The aim of this activity is to give some perspective and to enable children and young people to recognise that some problems can, in fact, be solved relatively easily.

Photocopy the 'problems' on the next page on card and cut them out. Give your group of students a selection of the 'problems' to discuss and to put in order from biggest problem to smallest problem. There are no right or wrong answers for this activity. What is more important is the discussion and awareness that some problems can be solved relatively easily, whereas others are more serious and longer-lasting. Students may also like to add problems that they can think of themselves, or you may choose problems that are more suitable for your group.

Discussion

Once students have ordered the problems, discuss possible solutions to them.

- Which problems can be solved relatively easily?

- Are there any which will be longer-lasting and require more support from other people?

Activity 17 'Big or little problem?' cards

Feeling bored at the weekend	A rainy day so you can't play outside with friends	Having to do a lesson you don't like
Getting no sleep and being very tired at school	Feeling frustrated at yourself for making a mistake	Something you were looking forward to being cancelled
Forgetting to bring equipment or homework to school	Being late to school	Getting into trouble at school
Getting into trouble at home	Feeling bored at break or lunch time	Having an argument with a friend
Parents splitting up	An elderly relative dying	Not understanding why you are in trouble
Being bullied at school	Not doing as well as you would like in a test or an exam	Not being able to do what you want at the weekend
Not knowing which option subjects to take	Having to speak in front of the class	Feeling lonely

Activity 18 My problems

Teaching notes

In this activity, students make a three-dimensional hot-air balloon. This is then used to demonstrate how various problems in the 'basket' can 'weigh you down' and make you feel low. Students can write their problems on pieces of paper which can then be folded and placed in the basket. Some students might find that this visual helps them to describe how they are feeling and demonstrate that a problem might be holding them down.

In Activity 35 the balloon analogy is used again to show what we can do to help ourselves feel better and 'fly high' again.

How to make a balloon

You will need:

- glue
- four short lengths of string or twine
- scissors
- one 'basket' template (see the next page), cut out of coloured paper or card
- four to eight 'balloon' templates, cut out of paper or card (the templates can be photocopied and enlarged to make bigger balloons).

What to do

1. Cut out the shapes you need on coloured or patterned paper or thin card.
2. Fold the balloons along the dotted lines and glue the backs of the balloon together. While doing this, glue the ends of the pieces of string between the backs of the balloons.
3. Make the basket and punch holes in each corner to tie the ends of the string through.

Activity 18 'My problems' hot-air balloon templates

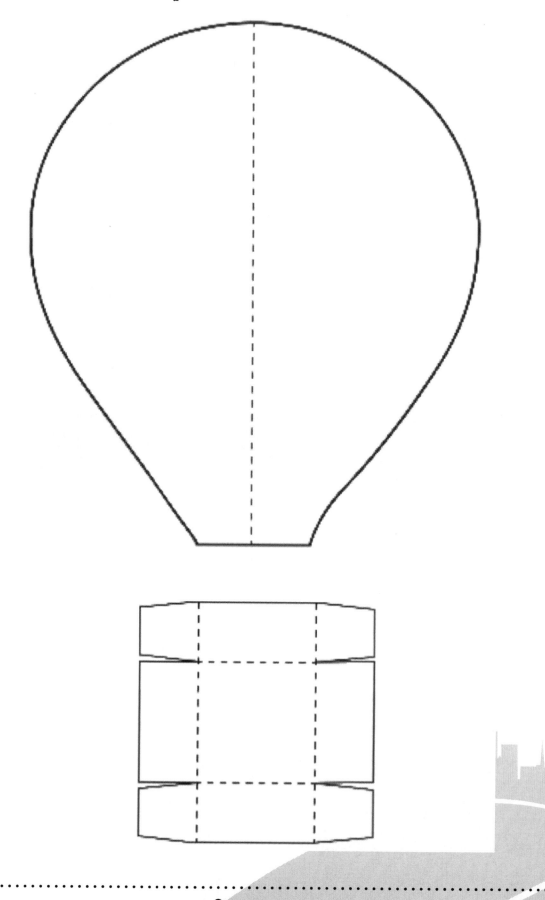

Speechmark Ⓢ

Activity 19 My worries

Teaching notes

All students are likely to have worries, whether big or small. Worries that we do nothing about can become bigger worries and go round and round inside our heads. This can mean that the worries become out of proportion and can begin to take over.

Some students may not feel comfortable talking about their worries, so this activity introduces the idea of a 'worry box'. The cube template on the next page can be copied, enlarged, assembled and decorated. Keep the lid open so that students can write down their worries and place them inside.

The 'worry box' can work in several ways. Students can write down their worries anonymously which are then discussed in the group. Alternatively, they can include their name and then an adult who has read their worry can approach them and discuss their concerns individually. A 'worry box' can help to reduce anxiety that students may have about approaching adults and asking for help.

Whole-school idea

The school, or individual classes, can have a 'worry box' or a confidential email or online form for students to report any concerns or issues. This can be a good way for students to feel they can report issues (such as bullying, or breaking of rules) confidentially and anonymously.

Activity 19 'My worries' box template

Speechmark

Activity 20 Body language

Teaching notes

Although feelings often appear to happen 'inside' us, we communicate these emotions and feelings through our facial expressions, body language, tone of voice and behaviour. This activity helps students to recognise how we experience and identify different emotions.

What to do

1. Choose a feeling word from the list below.

   - angry

   - shocked

   - nervous

   - guilty

   - excited

   - sad

   - happy

   - scared

   - confused

   - tired

2. Ask students to work in pairs to role play an example of somebody experiencing this feeling. Pictures or video clips could also be used to demonstrate this feeling.

3. Discuss the body language and facial expression associated with this feeling, the tone and volume of voice, and how we might behave. These can be recorded, in words or pictures, on the worksheet provided.

Activity 20 'Body language' worksheet

Feeling: _____

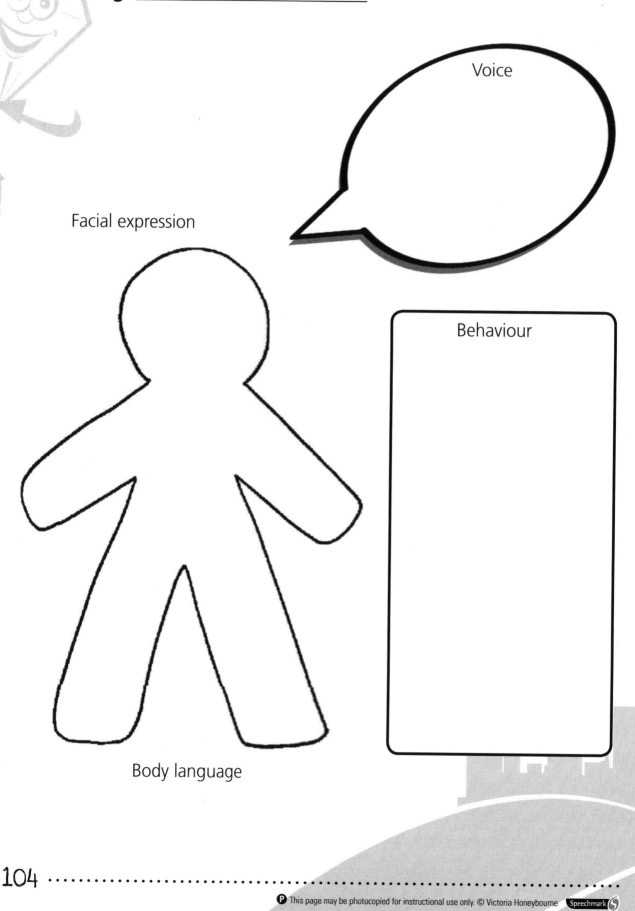

Voice

Facial expression

Behaviour

Body language

Activity 21 Name that feeling

Teaching notes

This activity supports students in recognising emotions in other people through demonstrating associated facial expressions and body language. The 'feelings' cards on the next page can be photocopied on card and cut out. Students take it in turns to pick a card and demonstrate that feeling without making any sound. They can create a 'freeze-frame' or mime. Other students then have to guess which feeling the 'actor' is portraying.

Discussion

- How did students recognise the feeling?
- What could they tell from the actor's facial expression and body language?
- Have they ever experienced a similar emotion?
- What was the situation?

Alternative

This activity can also be done by playing short video clips from films and television shows. Play the clip without the sound on, pause it and ask:

- What can you tell from the character's expression and body language?
- How do you think the character is feeling?

Activity 21 'Name that feeling' cards

happy	sad	disgusted	shocked	surprised
angry	afraid	scared	worried	hopeful
hopeless	guilty	embarrassed	enthusiastic	annoyed
bored	frustrated	cheerful	delighted	relieved
hurt	jealous	lonely	upset	pleased
sorry	proud	tense	uncomfortable	cross
grumpy	disappointed	excited	amazed	nervous
confused	depressed	anxious	frightened	tired

Activity 22 How are you feeling today?

Teaching notes

This activity can be used on a daily or weekly basis with students who would benefit. Each pupil can choose a 'character' from the next page to cut out and colour in. Alternatively, students may like to draw their own flying object (I have had bumble bees, unicorns, Pegasus, aeroplanes and magic carpets). Stick a small piece of Blu Tack™ on the back of each character.

The poster in Appendix 2 can be photocopied and enlarged. Students can then place their character on the poster to demonstrate how they are feeling that particular day. For example, they may place their character near the ground if they are feeling down, or higher up if they are feeling happier. Perhaps they feel like hiding behind a tree, or are stuck to the fence? Students can then be asked to explain why they have placed their character in a certain place which can then facilitate talking about how they are feeling that day and what could help them to feel better.

This can be a useful activity to do at the beginning of sessions or the start of the day as it can help to reduce worries and anxieties and solve problems before they become an issue.

Activity 22 'How are you feeling today?' characters

Getting on with other people

Getting on with people and enjoying satisfying relationships and friendships is essential to personal wellbeing. Martin Seligman (2002) observed that the happiest, most fulfilled people tend to be those who get on with others, enjoy company and have the most social relationships. The next set of activities focuses on friendships, getting on with other people and communicating assertively.

Learning that it is OK to talk about worries can be important for children and young people to recognise. Talking about a worry can help to shed light on the problem and help the individual see the issue from a different perspective. If you keep a worry in your head, it can grow and trouble you further. Talking is important in relationships as it can help to strengthen our ties with other people and help us to feel listened to and cared for (Mental Health Foundation, 2015). Often it can be beneficial simply to talk things through with family, friends or a teacher; in other cases, counselling by a trained professional may be more appropriate.

Activity 23 People who can help me

Teaching notes

This activity is designed to enable students to identify people in their lives who are able to help them. This can be the first step for students to recognise that there are many different people who can help in different situations.

Ask students to write the names of people who can help them on a copy of the chart on the next page. For example:

parents or carers	siblings	grandparents
extended family members	friends	classmates
neighbours	teachers	teaching assistants
other school staff	school nurse	doctor
social worker	counsellor	youth leaders

Discussion

Each pupil is likely to include different people on their chart. Some students might need support to generate a list of people. This activity can also be a useful opportunity to introduce students to various people within the school setting. Perhaps there is a school nurse, counsellor, mentor or student officer who students have not met yet? It can benefit some students to be introduced to these people personally. Information such as 'There is a school counsellor available on Monday lunchtimes in room 5' is not only likely to be forgotten quickly but also can be a scary prospect for students who may feel too shy or uncomfortable to approach new people.

Once the charts have been completed, explore with students who helps them with which things. For example, who would be most appropriate to help with homework, a sprained ankle, a family problem, or a friendship issue?

Whole-school idea

Invite your school nurse, counsellor or mentor to deliver assemblies or class activities so that all students are aware of the support available in school.

Activity 23 'People who can help me' chart

People who can help me ...

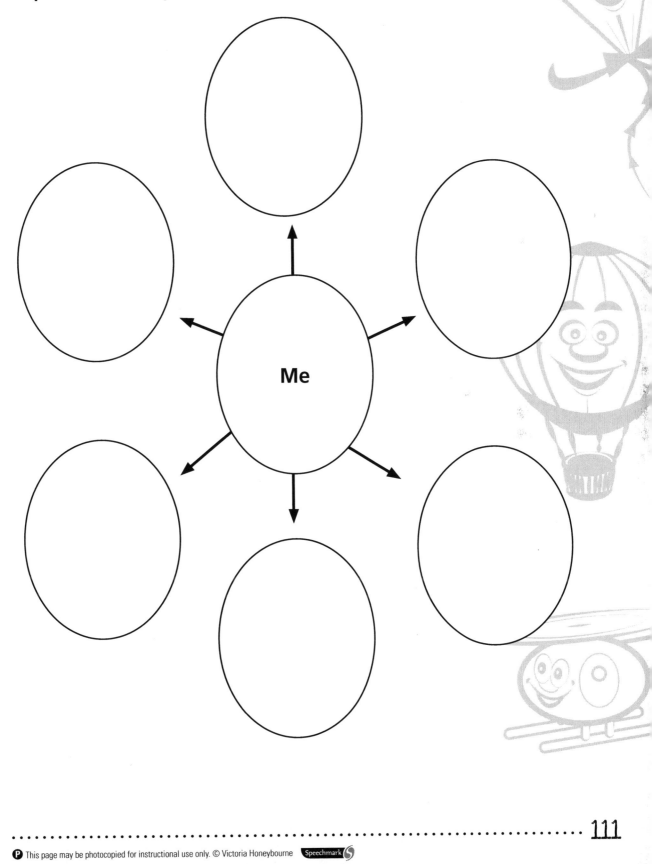

Activity 24 What makes a good friend?

Teaching notes

Friends are an important part of growing up. With friends we can take part in hobbies and activities we enjoy, talk through problems, learn new things, relax and have fun. Friendships can also cause misunderstandings, worry and stress, especially during the teenage years.

Discussion

Ask students what makes a good friend. These ideas can be recorded on a copy of the worksheet provided.

Use the following questions as prompts for discussion.

- Where can we make new friends?

- What can be difficult about making friends?

- Why are friends important?

- What makes a good friend?

- Do friendships last forever?

- What sort of problems might come up in friendships?

Activity 24 'What makes a good friend?' worksheet

What makes a good friend?

Activity 25 Asking for help

Teaching notes

For some students with special educational needs or communication difficulties, it can be difficult to know how to ask for help appropriately. This activity breaks down the process of asking for help into smaller stages.

What to do

1. Begin by talking through the checklist on the next page (Activity 25a). Do students understand why each step is important? Can they think of any examples (from real life or even from television) when people have or haven't followed these steps? What was the consequence?

2. Role play scenarios: Activity 25b consists of scenarios for students to role play or discuss. These can be photocopied on card and picked out at random. If you are working in a small group, students could work in pairs to prepare and act out a role play, with the other pair forming the audience and giving feedback.

3. Discussion: what went well in the way they asked for help? Could they improve it even further?

Whole-school idea

All students will need to ask for help with school work or school-related issues at some point. Encourage this by providing visual reminders around the school about where students can find help. This information could also be visible on your school's website and could include:

- staff in the school and what they can help with
- dates and times of revision sessions and extra-curricular activities on offer
- links to accessible websites
- useful books for homework.

Activity 25a 'Asking for help' checklist

What's important when you want to ask somebody to help you?

1. Make sure it is a convenient time. If the person is in the middle of doing something or is talking to somebody else, you may have to wait until they have finished. This will mean they can then concentrate on helping you.

2. Be polite. If you have to interrupt somebody, it is polite to begin with, 'Excuse me'.

3. Be clear and specific. It is useful if you can tell the person exactly what you need help with. This way they can help you more effectively. Both of these examples are polite, but which is most effective?

   a. 'Excuse me, Miss, I'm stuck.'

   b. 'Excuse me, Miss. Can you help me find a better word to use instead of "nice"?'

4. Say 'Thank you' when the other person has finished helping you.

Activity 25b 'Asking for help' Scenarios

Role play or discuss how you would ask for help in the following situations.

You would like to ask somebody at home to help you with your homework but everybody seems to be busy doing something.	You are in a café eating lunch and you would like to ask a member of staff where the toilets are.
You don't understand what to do in a lesson and want to ask somebody to help you.	You are at a train station and would like to ask when the next train is but the ticket seller is busy with a queue of people.
You fall over at lunchtime, have grazed your knee and feel a bit dizzy.	You are in a lesson and can't see the board because the light is shining on it.

Activity 26 Helping other people

Teaching notes

Research has shown that helping other people and carrying out acts of kindness can have a long-lasting feel-good effect (Seligman, 2003). Work by Sonja Lyubomirsky (quoted in Leimon & McMahon, 2009) also suggests that kind acts can give meaning to life, raise emotions to a positive state and increase happiness.

Use the discussion cards on the next page to encourage students to consider what they could do to help in each situation.

Further discussion

As a group, you could also discuss other acts of kindness and helpfulness. Ask:

- How do you feel when somebody helps you?
- Can you think of a time somebody was kind or helpful to you? What did they do?
- Can you think of a time you were kind or helpful to somebody else? What did you do?

Activity 26 'Helping other people' discussion cards

Your younger brother or sister is getting frustrated because they can't do their homework. • What could you do to help?	A teacher is trying to get through a door while carrying a large pile of exercise books. • What could you do to help?	One of your friends in class has forgotten her pen. • What could you do to help?
Your mum or dad is complaining that they have lots to do – washing-up, cleaning, and tidying the garden. • What could you do to help?	You have some old toys and some old clothes that don't fit you any more. • What could you do with them?	Somebody in your family has just come out of hospital and can't leave the house. • What could you do to help?
Your friend texts you because she has lost her homework sheet. • What could you do to help?	Your friend is upset because of something that has happened at home. • What could you do to help?	A new student has joined your class and is sitting by herself at lunchtime. • What could you do to help?

Speechmark

Activity 27 Talking to people

Teaching notes

Many children and young people with special educational needs can find it difficult to talk to others or maintain conversations.

Begin by discussing the 'rules of conversation' in Activity 27a. Why do students think that these things are important?

Activity 27b will demonstrate how conversations can 'go wrong'. Students can do this activity in pairs or with an adult. Other students in the group may like to observe and comment on what went wrong in the conversation.

Activity 27c practises 'quick conversations' – those conversations that take place with a range of people on a daily basis. It can be important for some students to learn social conventions for conversations such as these, and to learn appropriate topics to discuss in each situation.

Activity 27d explores topics that can be discussed in conversations with people we are closer to, such as friends, family and classmates. The group can discuss and add to these points, before role playing situations when they might make new friends and want to start up new conversations (eg when in a new class, or joining a sports club).

After these activities, students can then set themselves a target to work on during the next week (eg 'I will start up a conversation with the girl who sits next to me in art class', or 'I will look in the direction of the person who is speaking to me').

- How did they get on?

- What went well?

Activity 27a Talking to people

What makes a good conversation?

- Look at and listen to who is speaking.

- Take it in turns to speak.

- Wait until the other person has finished speaking before you talk.

- Ask when you have not understood something.

- Speak clearly and loudly enough.

- Respect other people's opinions.

- Stick to the topic.

- Ask questions to help other people join in the conversation.

- Change the topic appropriately.

Activity 27b Talking to people

When conversations go wrong

Photocopy the cards below and cut them out. Partner 1 takes a card from the first pile and partner 2 takes a card from the second pile. Follow the instruction on the card for two minutes. Then discuss:

- What went wrong?
- How did each of you feel?
- What could your partner have done differently?
- How would this have improved the conversation?

Partner 1

Talk to your partner about something that interests you.	Talk to your partner about what you did at Christmas.
Talk to your partner about what you did at the weekend.	Talk to your partner about your favourite lesson.
Talk to your partner about your ideal holiday.	

Partner 2

While your partner is talking, look around the room and fidget.	While your partner is talking, keep trying to change the topic to talk about something that you did recently.
While your partner is talking, stand up and walk around the room.	While your partner is talking, fidget, look around the room and pretend you are not interested.
While your partner is talking, keep interrupting and changing the topic	

Activity 27c Talking to people

Every day we might have conversations with people that are 'quick' conversations. In these conversations it is important to:

- Greet the other person appropriately.

- Be polite, use 'please' and 'thank you' when needed.

- Be clear and specific about what you want.

- Ask any questions that you need to.

- End the conversation politely and appropriately.

Copy and cut out the cards below. Work in pairs and role play the situation. The observers then comment on how well the 'actors' achieved each of the above points. What else could the 'actors' do to improve the conversation they had?

You are in a doctor's appointment as you have had earache for three days. One person takes on the role of doctor, the other of patient.	You are in the post office and want to enquire how much it costs to send a parcel to your friend who has moved to America. One person takes on the role of customer, the other of post office assistant.
You are in your local sports centre and want to go swimming. One person takes on the role of sports centre assistant, the other of customer.	You are ordering food in a restaurant. One person takes on the role of waiter, the other of customer.
You are in the waiting room at the dentist's and another patient starts up a conversation with you.	You are in your local library and want to ask for books about the First World War for a project you are doing. One person takes on the role of student, the other of librarian.

Activity 27d Talking to people

1. Complete the diagram below with more ways of starting a conversation with a friend or classmate.

Did you have a good weekend?

How to start a conversation

How are you?

I love that drawing you are doing.

2. What sort of things could you talk about with friends and classmates?

School events and activities

Topics to talk about

Hobbies

Music or TV

Activity 28 Assertiveness

Teaching notes

Being assertive is being able to tell other people how you feel and what you want respectfully and honestly. Being assertive is often seen as being on a continuum between aggressiveness and passiveness (see the table below).

Children and young people who are assertive can:

- resolve conflict to improve relationships
- take control of their own lives
- become more confident in their ability to achieve what they want
- be more likely to make positive choices
- be less likely to be victims of aggression or bullying
- be more able to say 'no' to peer pressure and behaviours that can harm themselves and others.

Passive	Assertive	Aggressive
A passive response involves saying or doing nothing, keeping your feelings to yourself and allowing others to treat you with disrespect. A passive response lacks confidence and avoids the problem.	Assertive behaviour involves expressing your thoughts and feelings honestly and openly to other people. It respects both yourself and the other person and allows you to exercise your personal rights without denying the rights of others.	An aggressive response can include sarcasm, put-downs, violence and anger. Other people are not respected. Aggressive behaviour involves attacking others either physically or verbally.

Begin with Activity 28a which introduces the ideas of passive, aggressive and assertive responses to children and young people.

Then, for each of the scenarios in Activity 28b, discuss the response. Is it effective? What would be a more assertive response to the situation? Students may like to role play the situations or create an animation or a photo story for the situation.

Discussion

Students can bring their own experiences to the discussion.

- Do they have examples of when they have responded to a situation aggressively or passively?
- What could they do differently to respond more assertively?

Activity 28a Assertiveness

When we are in a difficult situation we often respond in one of three ways:

Being assertive	You keep calm and use a low tone of voice. You use 'I' statements to describe how you feel (I feel … when you … because … . I would like … .) You look at the other person to show you are listening to their point of view. You respect other people's feelings and your own.
Being passive	You make yourself look small and may not look at the other person. You may speak quietly or not say anything at all. You go along with something even though you might not want to or you know it is the wrong thing to do. You act as if you are not as important as other people.
Being aggressive	You might shout, swear, threaten or hurt other people on purpose. You act as if you are better than others. You might stare at somebody, invade their personal space and not respect their feelings.

Activity 28b 'Assertiveness' Scenarios

What would be a more assertive response?

Somebody in the playground calls Jack a nasty name. He responds by punching them aggressively. What are the consequences for Jack? • What would be a more assertive response?	Beth is with some friends who get out some cigarettes and offer her one. She doesn't want to smoke but takes one and joins in, even though she doesn't like it. • What would be a more assertive response?
Amjad sees two older children bullying and threatening his friend. He pretends he hasn't seen it and does not tell anybody. • What would be a more assertive response?	Lily wants to get on with her work in class but her friend, Sunny, keeps bothering her and wants to chat. Lily tells Sunny to shut up and that she doesn't want to be friends any more. • What would be a more assertive response?
Sunita has lent her favourite pencil to a classmate who won't give it back to her. She starts crying and feels very upset. • What would be an assertive response?	Zac told a friend a secret about his family and his friend has told the whole class who are laughing at him. Zac swears at his friend and threatens to beat him up. • What would be a more assertive response?
Jamie's friends are teasing him about when he missed scoring an easy goal during a football match. They are trying to be funny but he is fed up with it now. He goes off by himself and starts to cry. • What would be a more assertive response?	Jacob wanted to do well on his homework but the teacher has pointed out some mistakes that he has made. He gets angry and shouts that it isn't his fault and he didn't understand what to do. • What would be a more assertive response?

Speechmark ✆

Using the positives

The final set of activities looks at how we can cultivate positive emotions and experiences. Research has shown that engaging in activities designed to develop a positive mindset can have a positive impact on wellbeing (Carr, 2011).

Activity 29 Gratitude

Teaching notes

A grateful person is aware of and thankful for the good things that happen. Learning to recognise and appreciate the good things in life can help individuals to experience joy from these good things and help to boost a sense of wellbeing. Many studies in which participants have been asked to 'count their blessings' have been shown to increase feelings of wellbeing (see Carr, 2011).

The first activity in this section is a 'Gratitude noticeboard' on which students are invited to record everything in their life they are grateful for, both past and present. These can be big or small things: this activity helps students to discover some of the good things in their life.

Here are some examples:

| My pet dog who I enjoy taking for walks. | Going to after school trampolining club. | Friends in my class at school. |

The second activity is a 'Things that went well' journal, inviting students to keep a diary for a week, looking for three things that went well each day. This activity can be continued over a longer period of time to help students recognise the positives that are happening on a daily basis.

Here is an example:

Day	Things that went well today
Monday	We had a visit from the guide dogs which was really interesting. One of my classmates said she really liked my drawings. I went to tennis club after school which was lots of fun. There was spaghetti bolognese for lunch – my favourite!

Discussion

- Did students find it easy or difficult to recognise the positives?

- Which things are going well?

- Are there any opportunities to build in more of these positive things?

- Which skills and strengths have students used to enable these things to go well?

Whole-school idea

Create a gratitude wall, or a 'Things that went well' wall, for students and staff to add to.

Activity 29 Gratitude noticeboard

Things I am grateful for ...

Activity 30 'Things that went well' diary

Day	Things that went well today
Monday	
Tuesday	
Wednesday	
Thursday	
Friday	
Saturday	
Sunday	

Activity 31 Relaxation

Teaching notes

Knowing how to relax effectively can be an important skill, especially in today's world in which many young people are constantly connected with modern technology and are often multitasking, flicking between screens and activities.

This activity is designed for students to explore activities which help them to feel relaxed, support them to feel calmer or help to distract them from worrying thoughts. Each individual will create a different list using the worksheet provided. This may include: sports, drawing, dancing, listening to music, crafts, sewing, walking the dog, reading, concentrating on breathing.

Discussion

- Why is it important to relax?
- How often do you do things that help you to relax?
- Could you do these things more often?
- What do you do when you are feeling upset or sad?
- Which other strategies would you like to try?

Good to know

It can be also useful to explain to students the benefits of concentrating on breathing mindfully. Concentrating on taking slow, deep breaths can help keep you focused and feeling grounded. When you are feeling angry or frustrated, concentrating on breathing for a few moments can help to make these feelings seem more manageable.

There are many resources available on mindfulness and meditation which can be effective ways of teaching young people how to relax and focus on the present.

Whole-school idea

Try offering a quiet room or relaxation space which all students can access if needed. Some children and young people find socialising exhausting and will benefit from having some time to themselves during the school day. Others may benefit from knowing that there is a safe space to use if they are feeling upset or want some alone time.

Activity 31 'Relaxation' worksheet

Things I can do to help
me relax …

Activity 32 Making mistakes

Teaching notes

It is important for children and young people to realise that we all make mistakes and have negative experiences, even as adults. Making mistakes is an inevitable and essential part of the learning process. It is often only by making a mistake that we can learn how to do things better in future.

Some students can be embarrassed by making mistakes or be sensitive to any implied criticism. They need to be reassured that it is a natural process to make mistakes and shown how most mistakes can easily be rectified. If children and young people are taught these skills, they can learn to feel more empowered to cope in these situations.

Useful mistakes!

In 1928, Sir Alexander Fleming, a British scientist who was trying to find a miracle cure for diseases, accidentally discovered penicillin, a powerful antibiotic, growing in a discarded Petri dish in his laboratory.

In 1968, Dr Spencer Silver, an American scientist working for the company 3M, was attempting to make a super-strong adhesive. Instead he created a super-weak glue which was not strong enough to stick things permanently. One of his friends used the mixture to stick a bookmark in his hymn book. Out of this 'mistake', sticky notes were created!

At the World Fair in 1904, an ice-cream seller ran out of cups and thought he could not sell any more ice-cream that day. Then the waffle seller next to him suggested rolling up a thin waffle and putting the ice-cream on top. Thus the ice-cream cone was invented!

Discussion

This activity involves using the scenario cards on the next page for students to discuss or role play. The cards can be cut out and students can discuss or role play the situations in pairs. They should aim to identify the most appropriate way of rectifying the mistake in question. For example, they could discuss:

- An apology. How could this be done sincerely and appropriately? Where and when is it best to apologise in each situation?

- If appropriate, how to rectify the mistake or solve the problem (eg by offering to clean up, or proposing a solution).

- What could be learned from the mistake or what could be done differently in future?

- Have students ever made similar mistakes?

- How does it feel to receive a sincere apology?

You could also make up your own scenarios that are relevant to your group of students.

Activity 32 'Making mistakes' scenario cards

Discuss or act out the situation on the card. How could the mistake be put right?

You are eating lunch and accidently knock over your friend's glass of juice. It spills all over the table. • What could you do?	You arrive in school and realise you have forgotten to do your English homework which is due that afternoon. • What could you do?
You give out invitations to your group of friends to come to your birthday party. The next day one of your friends isn't talking to you and you realise you accidently forgot to write her or him an invitation. • What could you do?	You get angry with a classmate who you think has taken the chocolate bar from your bag. When you get home, you realise that you had left it on the kitchen table. • What could you do?
You are annoyed with yourself as you found out that you did the wrong page in your workbook for homework. • What could you do?	You have forgotten to bring your PE kit to school. PE is your favourite lesson and you will also get a detention for forgetting your kit. • What could you do?

Activity 33 Finding the positives

Teaching notes

Psychological resilience can be seen as the ability to 'bounce back' after negative experiences. The psychologist Boris Cyrulnik (2009) found that positive emotions and humour are key factors in resilience and that people who can cope better with life's difficulties are able to view them as useful or enlightening experiences and even find ways to laugh about them.

Hope and optimism (looking forward positively) have also been found to benefit mental wellbeing. Hopeful and optimistic people have been shown to focus on success rather than failure, and believe that obstacles can be overcome (Carr, 2011).

What to do

This is an 'optimist versus pessimist' activity. For each scenario on the next page, allocate one student as 'optimist' and another as 'pessimist'. First, the optimist has to explain the situation from a positive point of view (what went well, good things that have come out of it, what has been learned). Then the pessimist explains the same situation negatively (why the situation is so bad, what has gone wrong). Students then discuss which would be the best view to take and what the consequences of each point of view could be.

For students who are not confident taking part in debate-style activities, these situations could be discussed as a group.

Discussion

Can students remember any negative experiences which have turned out to be positives or good learning experiences in the long term?

Activity 33 'Finding the positives' scenarios

You are doing work experience for a week in a shop. You are not enjoying it and decide you don't want to finish the week. You also decide that you don't want to do work experience next year and don't want to work when you leave school as you won't enjoy it.	You try out the after-school football club because you enjoy football. However, you find it difficult to talk to people and stand by yourself. You don't enjoy the club as you find it too lonely, so you don't think you'll try out any more after-school clubs.
Your class has been asked to give a presentation in front of the rest of the school. You think that is too scary, so you pretend to be ill to get out of doing it.	You were meant to be visiting a friend after school but you can't because she or he is feeling unwell. You go home and are bored.
You audition for the school play but you don't get the part you want. Instead you are given a smaller part as one of the dancers. You don't know whether to take the part or not.	You are very upset because you haven't done as well in your end-of-year exam as you had hoped.

Activity 34 Solving problems

Teaching notes

The next worksheet is a problem-solving template for students to use for a range of problems. It encourages students to identify the problem and possible options available to them, think about the pros and cons of each option and break down the chosen option into smaller, more manageable steps. This approach supports children and young people to focus on solutions and feel empowered to solve their own problems, rather than feeling that the problem is out of their control, or being dependent on other people.

Discussion

- Encourage students to be as specific as possible when identifying their problem.

- Support students to identify the pros and cons of each option and to verbalise their reasoning.

- Encourage students to break down their 'problem' into smaller, more manageable steps which they can achieve.

- Encourage independence in these problem-solving skills.

Students may need adult or peer support when completing this activity but, over time, they should be able to complete the template with increasing independence.

There is a completed example on the next page.

The problem I want to solve is …		
I don't know where to go for my work experience in the summer.		

My options	**Pros of this option**	**Cons of this option**
Option 1 I could go in to my mum's office with her for the week.	Easy to organise as my mum will do it.	I'm not interested in office work and working with my mum won't give me new experiences.
Option 2 I could ask the school if they have any animal care placements.	I might find a placement I will really enjoy. The school sorts out all the paperwork.	The placement might be far away from home.
Option 3 I could look for my own animal care placement.	I could find a placement close to home and doing something I enjoy.	I will have to write letters, make phone calls and send emails. The placements might say no.

I will choose option 2 because the school might have a suitable placement and if it doesn't then I will try option 3.

The steps I need to take to solve this problem are:

1 Ask for a meeting with the student work experience coordinator.

2 Explain that I would like a placement working with animals and that I can walk to/from home.

3 If they have a place, I will visit in advance to introduce myself.

4 I will ask what I will be doing, what I need to take and what time I need to be there.

Activity 34 'Solving problems' worksheet

The problem I want to solve is …

My options	Pros of this option	Cons of this option
Option 1		
Option 2		
Option 3		

I will choose option _____ because

The steps I need to take to solve this problem are:

1

2

3

4

5

Activity 35 Coping strategies

Teaching notes

Students by now should be able to see that there are many things that they can do to help themselves if they are feeling worried, down or anxious. This activity invites students to fill the 'balloon' on the next page with the strategies they would like to use to help them 'fly high' again, if a problem or worry in their 'basket' has pulled them down. Students can write or draw the strategies they would like to use, or have been using, in their 'balloon' and use this as a visual reminder of all the strategies at their disposal. This can be referred back to in future to remind students that they are in control of how they cope with difficulties.

Alternatively, students might like to use the hot-air balloon mobile which they created in Activity 18 and stick their strategies on the balloon.

Discussion

Students might add the following things to their 'balloon'.

Doing exercise

Doing a sport or hobby

Breathing slowly

Asking for help

Using a goal-setting sheet

Adding to my gratitude poster

Using the worry box

Doing things that I enjoy

Talking to somebody

Being assertive

Getting enough rest

Reading a book

Meditation

Using a problem-solving sheet

Looking at my memory wall

Thinking of 'three things that went well'

Remembering my achievements

Deciding whether it is a big or little problem

Spending time with friends

Learning from my mistakes

Eating well

Listening to music

Drawing

Accepting an apology

Apologising

Recognising the positives

Activity 35 'Coping strategies' hot-air balloon

Strategies I can use to pull me up when I'm feeling down

hot-air balloon

Appendices

Appendix 1
Teaching vocabulary

Many students with special educational needs or communication difficulties will need new vocabulary teaching explicitly and will need to revisit new vocabulary frequently. This appendix gives ideas of how to teach new vocabulary, followed by games to practise new words and a template for students to record what they learn. It is important for students to learn to define new vocabulary in their own words, rather than learn a dictionary or an adult's definition which can be meaningless and easily forgotten.

Learn the word	Hear it Say it Clap the syllables First sound? Last sound? Rhymes with?
Learn the meaning	Hear or read it in context Words that mean the same? Words that mean the opposite? Say it in a sentence Draw a picture of it Act it out Tell a story about it Define it (in your own words)
Remember it	Write it in your vocabulary book with a picture or definition in your own words Put it on your class word wall with a picture Play games with it

Vocabulary games

Bingo

Give students 'bingo cards', each with four to six items of key vocabulary on. Call out definitions; if a pupil has that word, they can cross it out. The first player to clear their card shouts 'Bingo!' and wins. The game can also be played by providing definitions and calling out the vocabulary.

Taboo

Make a set of cards, each one containing an item of key vocabulary. Students play in teams of two or more. A member of the first team picks a card and has to describe the word without saying the key word. Once somebody in the team guesses correctly, the player takes another card and moves on to defining the next word. After two minutes, the next team then takes a turn. The team which guessed the most correctly in the two minutes wins.

Match up

Ask students to match words with their definitions, or words with pictures. This can be done on an interactive whiteboard or as a paper-based activity. Words and definitions or pictures can also be made into 'dominoes' and played as a dominoes games. Alternatively, give some students in the class cards with vocabulary on and others cards with definitions. Can they find their 'partner'?

Charades

Charades can be played with many words, not just the traditional film and book titles. Students act out or freeze-frame a word and see whether other players can guess correctly.

Pictionary

Ask a pupil to draw an item of vocabulary. The rest of the group has to decide what is being drawn. The first person to guess correctly wins and takes the next go.

(Source: Mason & Milne, 2014)

My new word:

Draw what it means:

Write what it means:

Speechmark

Appendix 2
'How are you feeling today?' poster

Speechmark